GARGUNNOCK

Parish, Village,

and

G‹

Ian McCallum, B.E.M.

This book is dedicated to the memory of my grandmother Ellen Swan Hamilton, on whose knee I first heard all the old family legends. Also to my own future generations.

Acknowledgements

I wish to acknowledge the contribution made by a number of people. Without their encouragement and help this book would never have seen the light of day. Dr John Brims and Peter Clapham at Stirling County Archives for their patience and helpful suggestions. Elma Lindsay, Stirling Local History Officer for her interest in the project. Mary McIntyre at Stirling Library and Eric and Alice Dempster of McNair House, Gargunnock, for their tolerance and sense of humour while proof reading the early drafts.

A particular thank you is due to Mr John McLaren of Gargunnock, who not only contributed a number of the photographs and computer graphics, but made available his time and detailed local knowledge.

Acknowledgement is also due to the following organisations who gave permission to reproduce their material. The National Portrait Gallery, Sunderland Museum and Art Gallery, Halton-Deutch Collection, Gargunnock Kirk Session, Registrar General for Scotland and the Queen's Printer for Scotland, Trustees of the National Library of Scotland, Regimental Trustees of the Argyll and Sutherland Highlanders and the Trustees of the Stirling of Gargunnock Estate.

ISBN No. 0-9541263-0-0

Published by
Mr Ian McCallum, Trelawney Cottage, The Square,
Gargunnock, Stirling, FK8 3BH, Scotland
www.scottishancestors.co.uk

Front Cover
Gargunnock Main Street from the Manse Brae, looking west, c1855.
Reproduced with the kind permission of the Gargunnock Kirk Session.

Rear Cover
Trelawney Cottage (The Guest House) 2001

Printed by
The Monument Press, Abbey Road, Riverside, Stirling FK8 1LP

*This book has been produced by Jamieson & Munro
and production costs were supported
by a grant from the
Trustees of the John Jamieson Munro Charitable Trust*

CONTENTS

Page

List of Photographs, Maps and Drawings ... 5

Introduction ... 7
The Early Parish ... 10
Gargunnock and Prince Charlie ... 13
Gargunnock Kirk ... 19
Into the 18th Century ... 26
James McNair's Feu ... 35
18th Century Living Conditions ... 37
Conditions Improve ... 42
John Murdoch's House ... 50
The Nineteenth Century ... 52
The House 1849/65 ... 59
The Years of Decline ... 63
The Rev Stevenson and the Guest House ... 71

Appendices
I   Fallen of the Great War ... 78
II   Parish Ministers 1615-1888 ... 80
III   Parish Voters 1832 ... 82
IV   Members of the Gargunnock Farmers Club 1794 -1917 ... 84
V   Gargunnock Parish Ordnance Survey Place Names 1860 ... 91
VI   Summary of original and early feuars. ... 96
VII   Gargunnock early feu map ... 97
VIII   Gargunnock Parish National Census Return 1881 ... 98

Glossary ... 122

Weights and Measures and Currency ... 129

Source List and References ... 131

Bibliography ... 135

LIST OF PHOTOGRAPHS, MAPS AND DRAWINGS

Page

6   The Guest House c1955. From a photograph in the possession of the author.

13   Prince Charles Edward Stuart, by David. National Gallery of Scotland, Edinburgh.

14   Old Leckie House. Ancient Castles and Mansion of Stirling Nobility. Stirling Council Archives.

16   The old road from Stirling to Dumbarton and the tree under which the Prince Charlie and his Highland Army marched. From an original photograph in the possession of the author.

21   Archibald Marquis of Argyll. National Portrait Gallery, Edinburgh.

23   Gargunnock Kirk. From an original photograph by John McLaren.

27   Pamphlet issued by the supporters of William of Orange in 1689. Stirling Council Archives.

28   The arms of Sir James Campbell of Ardkinlass. From Ancient Castles and Mansion of Stirling Nobility. Stirling Council Archives.

29   A section of the Gargunnock estate plan of 1789, showing the early development of Gargunnock village. Stirling Council Archives.

31   The old packhorse bridge at Leckie Mill. From an original photograph by John McLaren.

32   The Moir of Leckie crest. Ancient Castles and Mansions of Stirling Nobility. Stirling Council Archives.

33   Old Gargunnock House. Ancient Castles and Mansions of Stirling Nobility. Stirling Council Archives.

39   Jean McAlpine's Inn near Aberfoyle.

43   The Gargunnock drum and trumpet, both now in the Smith Gallery in Stirling. From a photograph in the possession of the author.

45   A section of the Grassom map of Stirlingshire 1817 showing the parish boundaries. Stirling Council Archives.

47   The new mansion house of Leckie. From an original photograph by John McLaren.

51   The disposition document by which James McNair sold part of his feu to John Murdoch in 1798. The original is in the possession of the author.

54   A young girl dies of cholera in1832. Sunderland Museum and Art Gallery.

57   A coach and horses are stopped at a toll gate. The Hulton-Deutsh Collection.

58   Plan of Gargunnock Estate 1851. Stirling Council Archives.

60   A lance corporal of the 93rd of Foot. The original held in the Museum of the Argyll and Sutherland Highlanders (Princess Louise), The Castle, Stirling.

62   Water-colour of Gargunnock Village c1855 by M. S. Rownhill. Gargunnock Kirk Session.

63   McCulloch's house for sale in 1857. *The Stirling Advertiser*. Stirling Council Archives.

64   The Railway Station, Gargunnock. From a photograph in the possession of the author.

66   Main Street, Gargunnock c1890. From a postcard in the possession of the author.

68   Main Street, Gargunnock c1890. From a postcard in the possession of the author.

69   Brown's Public House for sale October 1900, *Stirling Journal and Advertiser*. Stirling Council Archives.

70   Children in the Square, Gargunnock, about 1906. From a photograph in the possession of John McLaren.

71   Portrait of the Rev Dr Robert Stevenson. Gargunnock Kirk Session

72   The Memorial Water Fountain and garden in the Square, Gargunnock. From a photograph in the possession of the author.

73   Public Water Supply ceremony 1910. From a postcard in the possession of the author.

75   Those recognised as being in the group photograph. Graphic produced by John McLaren.

77   The Guest House about 1906. From a postcard in the possession of the author.

78   The Memorial Scroll sent to the next of kin of the fallen of WW1. From a copy in the possession of the author.

81   Rev Mr John Stark, 1844-1888. The original is in the possession of Gargunnock Kirk Session.

90   The Square after the Guest House had closed, about 1918. From a postcard in the possession of the author.

95   Ordnance Survey 25" Stirlingshire, Gargunnock Parish, sheet xvi.4. 1860.

97   The original and early feus of Gargunnock superimposed onto the 1860 Ordnance Survey map of Gargunnock village. Graphic produced by John McLaren.

The Guest House 1955

The Guesthouse in the 1950s. The roof space has been broken into and the single loft room converted into two bedrooms. The stable on the eastern gable has also been converted and is now part of the house accommodation. In the mid nineteen seventies the old stable became the village post office, with Mr Gordon Matthews as the Postmaster.

Introduction

In an attempt to break away from the usual picture postcard type of village book, which shows the views and gives a short paragraph by way of explanation, I have set out an abridged history of the village and parish of Gargunnock, partly through the first hundred years or so of the life of an old house and the succession of owners and occupants who lived in it. However, while writing the history of the house, it quickly became apparent that the earlier history of the village and parish would need to be included to some degree. The idea originated with the bundle of old deeds belonging to the house which we received from our solicitors when my wife and I bought the property. Through these documents we can identify every owner of the house since it was built around 1798. The large house with green shutters, which stands on the eastern end of the terrace, over looking the water fountain in Gargunnock Square, has now been there for two centuries. The property was for a considerable time a drinking establishment, either a house where spirits could be bought, similar to an off license of today, or a public house or Inn. It was seldom simply a home and remarkably few children were ever raised in the property.

For the first hundred years or so, the owners seldom lived in the house, letting it out to sundry tenants and businessmen. One hundred years after it was built, it was converted from a public house called Brown's Pub into a Temperance Club called the Guest House. The latter is the name most natives of Gargunnock still associate with the property. In fact, the house was a Temperance Club for a fairly short period of time, only about 17 years, but the name has stuck. Various people then owned the property, for varying lengths of time, from the mid 1920s until the present. In the mid 1960s the then owners, Gordon and Doris Matthews, renamed the property Trelawney Cottage. In the mid 1970s Gordon ran the village post office from the single storey extension on the eastern gable, which had once been a stable.

Before we look in some detail at the history of the parish and village through the owners and occupiers of the house, we will look at the origins and history of both Gargunnock Parish and the village. The three, Parish, Village and House, represent three distinct phases in the evolution of the area and each has its own fascinating story to tell. The narrative ends in the years immediately after the First World War simply because the story of the village in particular could be better told by someone with a personal knowledge of the events and the characters involved, some of whose descendants are still living in the village.

Throughout this narrative I have drawn on many primary and secondary sources. Much of the information on the early history of the Parish and Village of Gargunnock comes from sources such as Moir of Leckie, Campbell of Ardkinlass, Eidingtoun and Stirling of Gargunnock family papers, 18th century agricultural reports, period newspapers, records of the 93rd Highlanders, maps, gazetteers, Monumental Inscriptions, Kirk Session Minutes and both the First and Second Statistical Accounts of Gargunnock of the 1790s and 1840s. I should probably explain something of the Statistical Accounts, which are such wonderful insights into the life and times of the late 18th and mid 19th century Scottish parishes. The aim was, with the co-operation of the 938 Parish Ministers, to survey the state of the country, through a series of one hundred and sixty six questions relating to conditions locally. The main questions covered the following topics: dress, food, fuel, customs, education, the poor, health, diseases, agriculture, fisheries, industry, occupations, population, parish history and religious matters.

The driving force behind the First Account was Sir John Sinclair MP of Ulbster, in Caithness, born in 1745. A major landowner and enthusiastic agriculturist, he founded the Board of Agriculture and became its first president. Only someone of Sir John's influence could have attempted such a project and could post over 800 letters and maintain a continuous correspondence over nine years with many of the participants. Being a Member of Parliament he could frank his own letters, overcoming the single biggest obstacle in mounting the project. The questionnaires were dispatched in May 1790 and the final replies were gathered in some nine years later.

On 3rd June 1799, Sir John presented the complete twenty one volume Account to the General Assembly of the Church of Scotland. The result is a detailed insight into the life and times of people who lived in the various Scottish parishes 200 years ago. Each parish Account is different and is a snapshot of life in the individual parish seen through the eyes of the minister. Often the character and interests of the ministers themselves shine through. For example, if he was interested in zoology, then that section of the account is detailed and written with passion, sometimes to the detriment of other topics. The Reverend James Robertson arrived in Gargunnock in 1787 and he submitted a very detailed, well balanced account of the parish. He was to remain as minister for seventeen years, transferring to South Leith Parish in December 1804.

Fifty years later the process was repeated, again the ministers were required to answer questions relating to their parish. The minister in Gargunnock for this second account was the Reverend James Laurie. Taken together both Accounts present a very detailed picture of the lives of the parishioners of Gargunnock over a period of 80 years or so. We owe an enormous debt to the many generations of Ministers, Session Clerks and Elders of the Kirk for the records and accounts which they left to posterity. The Scottish nation is indeed fortunate to have such a wealth of primary historical information at its finger tips. A third Account was published in the 1960s.

The history of the house itself is based mainly on the original deeds and other legal documents in my possession, extracts from the Old Parish Registers, Statutory Records, National Census returns, Tax Records, Valuation Rolls and early photographs.

Finally, before we look at the history of the Parish and Village and without going in too deeply, an explanation of the Feudal system of land ownership might be helpful as it at one time formed the basis for all land transactions, around which most other facets of the parishioners life once revolved. The feudal system was brought to England by William the Conqueror and the Normans after 1066 and was later introduced to Scotland by King David I. Very simply, the system could be thought of as a pyramid, with the king at the top. It assumes that the king owns all the land and in return for their support both militarily and financially, the king allocated vast tracts of the country to a few of the highest noblemen, dukes and earls and until the Reformation, the Church. These magnates would in turn allocate portions of their vast holdings to nobles of lesser rank, barons for example, again in return for military and financial support. These minor nobles were the lairds, usually some relation to the magnates, younger sons or cousins perhaps. From around the 16th century a system called Feuferme became popular. This saw the introduction of small landowners not of the nobility who were known as feuars. These small farmers generally worked their 20 or 30 acres alongside their labourers and were commonly known as Bonnet Lairds. In the 18th century, in response to changing agricultural working conditions, feudal superiors began to make much smaller feus available as individual plots of ¼ and ½ acre sites on which fairly humble individuals could build houses.

All these landowners were required to pay various types of duty to the person from whom they held their land and who was termed their Feudal Superior. In some cases the lairds could hold their land directly from the Crown, as was the case with Leckie and Gargunnock Baronies. Not part of the feudal land-owning classes, beneath these landowners on a sliding social scale were the tenant farmers, then small crofters, cotters and grassmen, all working on the land for the laird, bonnet laird or tenant farmer, as ploughmen, herdsmen, threshers etc, usually in return for a rented cottage and small patch of ground, on which they could grow some crops and graze an animal. These people were probably tenants at will and appear to have had little or no security of tenure. At the very bottom of the social pile were landless labourers and indoor farm servants, people who worked around the farm in return for their keep. Sometimes they lived and ate with the farmer or 'Guidman' or later they might live in a bothy or hut nearby. They could also be the wives, younger sons and daughters of crofters and cotters working off part of the family rent on their parents' or husbands' behalf, under a system known as Bondage. They were particularly useful at harvest time when lots of extra hands were required. Vestiges of the old feudal system of land ownership remained in general use until very recently. Some of the more detailed points concerning land tenure will be looked at later in the narrative.

At the rear of the book is a number of appendices, including the 1881 Gargunnock Parish National Census Return and map of the original 18th century village feuars showing their properties. The appendices have been included to assist those readers researching their Gargunnock ancestors.

Ian McCallum,
Gargunnock.
March 2001.

The Early Parish

The name of the parish is believed to be Celtic in origin and is derived from the words Caer and guineach, meaning a sharp or conical fortress. The Peel or fort of Gargownno, as it is sometimes called in the oldest records, once stood guard over a ford at the junction of the Forth and the Gargunnock Burn, at a place known locally as the Poo Mooth. The parish of Gargunnock is situated five miles west of Stirling and on the south side of the river Forth which is also its northern boundary. Its western and south western boundaries are the Boquhan Burn and the Backside Burn. On the east it is a small stream between Redhall Farm and West Carse Farm. To the south east the boundary is the Burnfoot Burn. The area to which it gives its name extends about four miles from east to west, and about five miles north to south. Geologically, it can be divided into three distinct parts, moorland, dryfields and carse.

The moorland is on the south of the parish and consists of the high country of the Gargunnock and Lennox Hills. It is typical heather and bracken covered land and was never widely cultivated, but used for grazing sheep and black cattle in the summer months. Few people ever lived there permanently, only the occasional family of shepherds or cattle drovers.

The dryfields lie between the moorland and the carse and as the name suggests, because of the gentle slope and very light sandy soil, water is either absorbed or quickly runs off the land. These dryfields were once considered the best ground before the carse was drained and the peat removed. This was the area on which the majority of the people once lived, mostly in small farms and fermtoun communities. The organisation and way of life of the fermtouns will be explained in greater detail later. The village of Gargunnock grew up on the slopes of the dryfields, near where they meet the carse.

The carse land itself lies to the north of the parish on a flat plain, the northern border of which is the River Forth. Once covered in thick peatbog, this area is now among the most fertile land in the country, though still subject to temporary flooding in prolonged periods of heavy rain. Believed once to have been under water as part of a much wider River Forth, or of a sea loch, beds of shells similar to ones found on the Firth of Forth have been found in several places. When the sea loch or river receded, part of the ancient Caledonian forest covered the area. The area of the forest was cut down by Roman legionnaires about the 3rd century. The marks of their axes have been found on trunks of felled trees uncovered when excavating the carse. For the next thousand years or so a thick layer of peat grew over the carse lands, in some places to a depth of 15 feet. By the mid 18th century, the agricultural improvements sweeping the country saw the peat layer removed and a wonderfully fertile plain develop.[1] The carse was always occupied and slightly higher areas cultivated, mostly by farmers renting very small areas of a dozen or so acres, who would have waged a constant battle against flooding.

Politically, the parish was split into three ancient Baronies, Leckie, in the centre, Boquhan on the west and Gargunnock on the east. A Barony was an area of land granted by the crown to a tenant in chief and was in itself a social and economic unit with the right to hold periodic markets and fairs. The Baron or Laird, was generally the Feudal Superior of the land and was an immensely powerful figure, not only had he the power to evict tenants from their homes he had the power of life and death, quite literally, over the people who resided on his lands. The Laird himself or his Baillie presided over the Barony Court and had the power to settle civil disputes and to fine, imprison and even execute for criminal offences. To assist the court a number of tenants called Birlawmen would sit as a jury. These men were the older, more experienced tenants, whose considered judgement those in dispute, including the Laird, would accept. Towards the end of the 17th century the courts were mainly concerned with settling disputes within the old agricultural system of communal farming. However, Feudal Superiors were still exercising their right of Pit and Gallows as late as 1693, when the Viscount Kilsyth hung one of his house servants for the theft of silver plate. The fellow was executed in the Barony of Bancloich, at a place called Gallowhill.[2] The system of Birlawmen being used as mediators and honest brokers was still in operation in Leckie barony well into the 19th century. In 1813, Dr Moir of Leckie called three such men, John Murdoch, William McEwan and Duncan Lockhart, to make judgement as to fair repairs to a steading at Patrickstown, prior to it being leased.[3] The area to the east of the village at the top of the Manse Brae, was once known as Courthill and may have been the meeting place of the old Barony or Birlaw Courts.[4]

Throughout the narrative we talk about the baronies of Gargunnock, Leckie, Boquhan and the estates Meiklewood, Kipdarroch, Culbeg and the likes. We must remember that these lands were continually changing hands, with parts of this estate and bits of that estate, being attached or detached from the others in the area. The landed families almost always married into their own class and lands which came as dowries with the brides were absorbed into the estate of the husband, only to be given away a couple of generations later as their own daughters or granddaughters were married. The borders which we assign to these areas today have only come into being during the 19th century.

The land records of 1470 show the Barony of Gargunnock as being in the possession of among others, Alexander Hepburn and his wife Marote Normanvil, styled the *"Laidy of Gargunok"*. This line of Hepburns failed in the next generation and the lands of Gargunnock were split between two daughters. Margaret Hepburn sold her part to Lord Elphinstone in 1511. The other sister, Marjory, died unmarried in 1531 and her estate reverted back to the crown. A year before she died, under the name *Marjory Hepburn Lady of Gargunnock*, she gave a grant of the 1 merk lands of Kipdarroch to Alexander Leckie, which suggests her part of the lands lay next to Leckie.[5] In 1513 Ninian Seton of Touch gained possession of one sixth of the Gargunnock lands which included the tower fortalice and manor.[6] The oldest part of the present Gargunnock House is the east wing with its corner turret and walls which are 4 feet thick. The old structure was once surrounded by an outer wall and stout gate dating back to this period.[7]

In 1570, the Setons of Touch also gained the 15 merk land of Gargunnock, which included the Mill, and had aquired part of Meiklewood. Sometime between this date and 1624, the Setons of Touch and Tullibody sold or disposed of Gargunnock, including the tower fortalice and manor to the Erskine Earls of Mar.[8] The confiscation of the church lands of Gargunnock during the Reformation added to the possessions of Mar. By 1675, the Gargunnock lands had been feued by a family of Campbells who in 1707, settled the lands on James Campbell of Ardkinlass when he married their daughter Margaret. The lands remained with this family until the end of the 18th century.[9] The baronies of Leckie and Boquhan followed the same pattern of land acquisition and subsequent disposal. The local landowners of the early to mid 19th century through various land deals tidied up the Barony and estate marches, finally creating roughly the boundaries we see today.

The area around the present village square has been occupied continuously for a considerable period of time. Keir Hill, immediately to the south of Gargunnock bridge was partially excavated by the Royal Commission on Ancient Monuments in the late 1950s. This showed that there had been early human dwellings on the crest of the hill. The dwellings, which were circular in shape surrounded by wooden posts and flagged inside with stones laid on the ground, were destroyed by fire some time between 50 and 100 A.D. The site was fortified in the 13th century and the mound which is oval had at one time been surrounded by a rampart.[10]

Historically, no events of any great significance took place in the parish itself. However, its proximity to the vitally strategic Stirling Bridge and to the Ford of Frew, for centuries the first crossing point above Stirling Bridge, and sitting as it does astride the main route from Stirling to Dumbarton, meant it witnessed the comings and goings of many of the major players in the history of the nation.

During the Scottish Wars of Independence Sir William Wallace sallied forth from the ancient fortress on Keir Hill, stormed the Peel of Gargunnock and killed its English garrison. Sir William later met a gruesome death at Smithfield in London, but Robert Bruce picked up the gauntlet and won freedom for the nation at Bannockburn in 1314. Both Keir Hill and the Peel get a mention in the medieval account of the times by Blind Harry. In the same troubled period the lands of *Leky* were Crown property until Bruce gave the western portion nearest Boquhan to Malcolm 5th Earl of Lennox in exchange for a Lennox property at Cardross, in Dunbartonshire, where Robert Bruce died in 1329.

In July 1545, when the infant Mary Queen of Scots was lodged in Stirling Castle, John, Laird of Lekky was entrusted with the safe keeping of the child. John Lekky of that Ilk and many of his clansmen drawn from the lands of Leckie, were to die fighting for their queen at the Battle of Pinkieclough, near Musselburgh in September 1547, when 23,000 Scots were routed by an English force which utilised naval gunfire.[11]

One battle did take place in the parish and again it involved the Leckies. A great feud between the Leckies and the Grahams of Menteith began about 1575. The cause of the feud has been lost, but in March or April 1577 a clan battle took place at Ballochleum (the Pass of the Leap) a gorge down which the Boquhan Burn falls on the western extremity of Gargunnock parish. The result of the battle and casualties sustained, like the cause of the feud, have been lost. Unlike the Leckies who were a fairly small tribe holding a single Barony, the Grahams were a large powerful clan with possessions and family connections throughout the central lowlands and east coast. The matter came to the attention of the Privy Council in Edinburgh and was noted in the Minutes;

"Forsamekill as upon licht and slendir occasion unhappily fallen out, there wes diverss slachters committit betwext the friends, servants, and dependants of William Earl of Menteith and Walter Lekkie of that ilk … assurances were given

*and persons denounced rebels relaxed in hope of some concord and quietness
in the country to have followed, howbeit sensyne the former trubill and misrule
has been renewit and slachter lately committit, whereupon fude inconvenient is
likely to follow if timeous remeid be not povidit, therefoir ordains letter to be
directit charging baith the said parties to compear personally before the Lord
Regent and Secret Council on the last day of May to answer sic things as
salbe inquired of them and to underly sic ordour and directions as salbe
imputed to them under pane of rebellion and putting to the horn.*

Despite the instructions and threats from the Privy Council, thousands of merks
paid in sureties from both parties and later threats from the king himself, the feud
grumbled on for another twenty years.[12]

Gargunnock and Prince Charlie

Over 400 years after Bruce, a descendant, through
his daughter Marjory and her husband Walter
Stewart, led an army through the parish. On Friday
13th September 1745, Prince Charles Edward Stuart
and his Highland host crossed the River Forth at
the Ford of Frew. Traditionally, it is said that the
Prince breakfasted at Boquhan and slept at Leckie.
This was not the case. The then Laird of Leckie,
George Montgomery Moir, a staunch supporter of
the Jacobite cause, was preparing to welcome his
Prince. However, government spies intercepted a
letter he sent to his prince inviting him to Leckie.
The spies informed the local Hanoverian commander and the night before the Prince was due,
while the Laird and his family were in bed, a
troop of government dragoons seized the Laird
and took him a prisoner to Stirling Castle, where he
languished for the next two years.[13] Prince Charles
duly arrived at Leckie and in her husband's absence

Prince Charles Edward Stuart.

was entertained to dinner by Anne Montgomery, mistress of the house. It was from
Leckie Castle that the Prince addressed his famous demand to the magistrates of
Glasgow for £15,000 and whatever arms were to be found in the city.

Although local legend states that the Prince slept at Leckie, the Prince and his
army in fact passed the night of the 13th at Touch, on the eastern edge of the
Parish. The Laird of Touch at the time was Hugh Seton, who although a Jacobite,
had shrewdly decided to be absent from the county during the rebellion. The
embryonic village of Gargunnock would therefore have witnessed the Bonnie
Prince and his Highlanders, led by their pipers, march along the road from Leckie,
down the village main street, over the old bridge, past the Kirk and on towards
Gargunnock House, where they marched under the branches of an ancient
chestnut tree and on to Redhall, Touch and the south. In those days the line of
the old road took it much closer to Gargunnock House. The old chestnut tree stood
in the grounds of the house in the early 1960s.[14]

Old Leckie House

Old Leckie House much as it would have appeared to Charles Edward Stuart when he visited in 1745.

It is difficult to ascertain exactly how much support there was for the rebellion in the Parish. A number of the local landed families were supporters and normally their tenants would follow their laird. However, although many lairds supported with their hearts, few supported with men or money. The Laird of Gargunnock at the time was Sir James Campbell of Ardkinlass, one time governor of Stirling Castle, who like Seton of Touch, made a point of not being at home when the Prince called. The Campbell Clan and its septs for the most part supported the government, though curiously the Jacobites put an armed guard of Cameron clansmen on Gargunnock House to prevent it being pillaged. The commander of the guard was Alexander Cameron of Dungallon, who was a cousin of Colin Campbell of Glenure. Alexander Cameron surrendered after the Battle of Culloden and later at his trial, cited guarding Gargunnock House as a point in his favour. Cameron survived the treason charge and was discharged from Edinburgh Tollbooth in October 1749.[15]

The Protestant Church of Scotland of course opposed the Catholic Prince Charles Edward and the minister of Gargunnock at the time, William Warden, would have preached vehemently against any involvement with the papist rebels. The Kirk of 1745, promising eternal damnation, held its parishioners in a powerful grip. The Highland army passed over the ford at Frew again during their retreat north on 1st February 1746, but on this occasion there was little time for socialising, with the Hanoverian forces in pursuit. This time, in the confusion of the retreat, the Jacobites left cannon and equipment behind at Leckie. On the two occasions that Prince Charles and his army passed through Gargunnock, few of the parishioners would have been there to greet them; the inhabitants would have been terrified for their lives and possessions. Having been warned of the Highlanders' approach, most including any local Militiamen, would have gathered what little food and valuables they had and headed for the safety of Stirling or the hills, driving their beasts before them.

A contemporary description of the behaviour of the Highland Army when it entered the parish, can be found in the Metrical History of the Rebellion by the Stirlingshire poet Dougal Graham.

> And at the Frew they crossed the Forth, the only passage from the north;
> Without the help of boats or brigs, Charles himself first wet his legs;
> Being on the front of all his foot, for help of horse there sought he not;
> And on the south bank there he stood, till all of them had passed the flood;
> Here for a space they took a rest, and had refreshments of the best;
> The country round them could afford, though many found bit empty board;
> As sheep and cattle were drove away, yet hungry men sought their pray;
> Took milk and butter, kirns and cheese, on all kinds of catchables, they seize;
> And he who could not get a share, sprang to the hills like dog for hare;
> There shot the sheep and made them fall, whirl'd off the skin and that was all;
> Struck up fires and boiled the flesh, with salt and pepper did not fash;

The clan chiefs did attempt to keep their followers in check and Dougal Graham describes how Cameron of Locheil shot one of his followers whom he caught pillaging.

> This did enrage the Cameron's chief, to see his men so play the thief;
> And finding one in to the act, he fired and shot him through the back;
> Then to the rest himself addressed, "This is your lot, I do protest;
> Who e'er amongst you wrongs a man, pray what you'll get, I tell you plain;
> For yet we know not friend or foe, nor how things may chance to go."

15

The Old Road

A late 19th century photograph of the old road and tree under which Prince Charlie and his Highlanders marched en route to Touch. Relatively untouched, it gives a good indication of the state of the roads of the time. The tree stood in the gardens of Gargunnock House until the mid 1960s.

There is a couple of versions of this incident and the burial of the slain Highlander. One version is that while the prince and his chieftains were dining at Leckie house, a local woman complained that the Highlanders were stealing her sheep. The chief of the McGregors said "that will be the Camerons". The young Cameron chief, Locheil, said "no, its more likely to be McGregors". After laying a bet, both chieftains loaded pistols and went to find the offenders. They soon came across a Cameron Highlander with a sheep across his shoulders, Lochiel immediately shot him. The dead man was carried to Seton of Touch's carpenter, who as a staunch Hanoverian refused to make the coffin. Another local carpenter was eventually found, who, having sympathies for the Jacobite cause, made a coffin and the Highlander was buried at Bridge of Millburn on the Touch estate. When the Laird of Touch arrived back on his estate and heard the tale, he dismissed the first carpenter and gave the position to the second.

Most of the Jacobite army spent the night on the Moor of Touch, but some troops were quartered in the nearby villages. There is a possibility therefore that some of the Highlanders remained in Gargunnock as opposed to simply marching through. The Jacobite commanders decided to avoid Stirling and to make straight for the Scottish capital, by way of Cambusbarron, Falkirk and Linlithgow. After capturing Edinburgh and six weeks after their victory at Prestonpans on 21 September 1745, the victorious prince marched his Highlanders into England determined to regain the British throne for his father. Only 5 weeks later on the 6 November, lack of English support forced the Highland Army to retire having reached Derby, only 130 miles from London. The army retired by way of Carlisle which they reached on 19 December. By 24 December they were quartered on the town of Hamilton. Another detailed account of the behaviour of the Jacobite troops follows, though it should be remembered that letters of this kind were often used as propaganda:

"We have got a visit from your formally troublesome neighbours, which we neither expected, desired or wanted. However, their stay was but short; but at the same time very troublesome. Upon Tuesday the 24th of December, in the afternoon there came here, 1900 horse and foot, tho they gave themselves out as 2500. They were commanded (If I may call it so) by the Lords George Murray, Nairne, Elcho, Ogilvie and Glenbucket and others. Upon the Wednesday morning, part of them went off for Glasgow; and that afternoon their Prince, the Duke of Perth, their French ambassador and others, with parts of their clans came in. Both these nights the people of the town, tho greatly thronged, were at greater peace than on the Thursday night when the Camerons, MacPhersons and MacDonalds of Clanranald's party came up, after burning houses in Lesmahagow, and rifling one of the minister's houses; and had it not been for Lochmoidart's brothers, they would have laid the whole town in ashes and plundered the country roundabout, and then indeed we felt the effects of an undisciplined, ungovernable army of Highland robbers who took no more notice of their nominal prince, or commanders than a pack of ill bred hounds.

The provisions, ale and spirits beginning to run short in the town, they threatened the people with death, or the burning of their houses, unless such victuals and drink were got as they called for; which victuals were not of the coarse sort, Herrings, onions, butter and cheese, which we looked upon as best food, such they would not take. The people of England have taught them such a bad custom, that they would scarce taste good salt beef and greens. The meanest of them were calling for roast or fried fresh victuals; if such were not got they treated the people very ill. My lodgers were so luxurious they would not taste boiled pork, a little pickled, without it first being fried in butter. Among this set of ruffians were some civil people, some of whom my aunt and her two neighbours had the good fortune to get for lodgers. I had no less than 33 of them, the last night, of the worst kind, besides horses and naked whores. Our subscribers, volunteers and militia, were obliged to leave the place, among whom were your good brother and myself, so I had not the trouble of them, tho their three nights lodging, with what they stole from me, cost me about six pounds sterling. They have rifled several houses in the neighbourhood and broke or destroyed what they could not carry off, particularly at Captain Crawford's, Thomas Hatton's at Smiddycroft and Woodside.

The prince went hunting upon Thursday, in the Duke's park; he shot two pheasants, two woodcocks, two hares, and a young buck, all of which were carried in triumph. He dined at Chatleroy, where I saw him, but could not find this angel – like Prince among the whole rabble, till he was pointed out to me. While here they stripped the people of their shoes upon the street, and took what they thought proper for them, refusing to be hindered in any way by their officers.

There was not any of this rabble, but what were possessed of plenty of gold, even the smallest boys, and nakedest whores. We were freed from these troublesome neighbours upon Friday morning the 27th, who left us nothing but innumerable multitude of vermin, and their excrements; which they left not only in our bed chambers, but in our very beds. The civilest kind held their doups over the stock of the beds, like crows shiting over the nest. Our town smells of them yet, but the people's spirits are getting up, for while they were here, they looked like dead corps. They stopped us from a merry Christmas, but God be thanked, we were blessed with a merry new years day. I wish you a happy new year and peace, which we now begin to learn to value. All friends being here assembled, join in good wishes and services to you.

I am &c.
Hamilton 6th January 1746.[16]

By 3rd January 1746, the Jacobites were at Stirling where they laid siege to the castle, held for the government by Major General Blackney. On 17th January, the Highlanders defeated a Hanoverian force at Falkirk, however, they failed to press home their advantage and instead moved back to Stirling where they resumed the siege. The Highlanders were not suited to siege warfare and during the lull in activities they began drifting away back over the Forth, many laden with booty. By the end of January, the Duke of Cumberland and a government army was at Linlithgow. The seriousness of the situation was impressed on the prince and he reluctantly agreed to retire northwards on 1st February. The Jacobite army's supposed tactical withdrawl became a fiasco and more like a rout, as undisciplined hoards of Highlanders streamed back through Gargunnock towards the Ford of Frew in total disorder. One of their commanders complained that not a thousand marched together. Advance parties of government troops began harrying the retreating Highlanders, dealing summarily with any they caught. Again, Dougal Graham describes the scene.

> *The Campbells and some troops of horse, that night arrived at Stirling cross;*
> *Who came harassing the retreat, and picked up stragglers by the gate;*
> *Blackney also sallied out, and catch'd some strollers thereabout;*
> *Many of them were so mischiev'd, it shocked nature to perceive;*
> *Legs and arms shot clean awa, and some wanting the nether jaw;*
> *Some were out of trenches drawn, being buried alive midst the san;*
> *The Campbells kept upon the chase, and picked them up in many a place;*

Some canon were found near the Frew, their horse being weak could not go through;
Much baggage left and several things, with a printing press, called the King's;
Which back to Stirling was returned, while Charles, by Crieff to Perth adjourned.

At about one o'clock on 1st February 1746, Prince Charles Edward Stuart ate his last meal in the Lowlands of Scotland, when at Boquhan he and his officers sat down to lunch. The highly confused military situation and an example of the split loyalties in the parish can be illustrated by the fact that the night before the Prince crossed the Forth, a party of government soldiers arrived at the farm of Robert Forrester of Wester Frew. The commander, Captain Campbell, asked Forrester to show him the ford. The farmer's sympathies lay with the Jacobites and suspecting Campbell was up to something, showed him to another minor ford nearby the Frew which was seldom used. Campbell immediately ordered his soldiers to throw caltrops into the water and withdrew back towards Stirling. The next afternoon Prince Charles arrived at the ford and while his large euenerauge took to the Forth at the Ford of Frew, the prince crossed at the minor ford and had his horse spiked by the caltrops.

The departure of the bulk of the Highlanders from the parish would have allowed the Gargunnock Militia to reform, probably having dispersed while the Jacobites were in the area in strength. On 7th February 1746, they captured four Jacobite soldiers, two carrying arms. The stragglers had probably been in hiding for days, having been caught out by the speedy arrival of government troops. Perhaps they were walking wounded or perhaps had been attached to the prince's baggage train at Leckie. The Edinburgh jail register for 1746, now in the National Library of Scotland, shows the four rebels were dispatched from Stirling to Leith and onto Edinburgh where they handed over to the Cannongate jail on the 24 June 1746. Unlike in the Highlands where Hanoverian retribution was swift and harsh, few Lowland Jacobite sympathisers were punished. Those parishioners who had secretly or otherwise supported the King over the water, wisely decided to get on with life under the current regime and Gargunnock's association with the Bonnie Prince and national politics was over.

Gargunnock Kirk

The Church has always been at the very heart of the parish and the present Kirk building stands on the same site as a number of its predecessors. The original Gargunnock Church was founded by the medieval monks of Cambuskenneth Abbey and was a pendicle of St Ninian's in the mid 16th century.[17] The use of the site for a religious building probably goes back much earlier than that considering that it once sat astride one of the major routes to the west from Stirling, which was at one time Scotland's capital.

During the episcopal regime of the early 17th century Gargunnock came under the jurisdiction of the See of St Andrews, until 1633 when the lands south of the Forth were transferred to the Bishop of Edinburgh.[18] The Kirk building was regarded by the Kirk Session as being in a ruinous state in 1626. Six years earlier they had been promised money from the Gentlemen and Heritors of the parish to build a new Kirk.[19] There is no evidence of any wanton destruction or accidental damage having been done to the building and therefore a ruinous building in 1620 suggests a structure at least 100 years old, which would take the origins of that building back to well before the Reformation of 1560. This pre-Reformation building was subsequently rebuilt at least twice. First in 1628, when a rectangular structure extending east-west was erected. The Kirk and new dyke had been rebuilt with donations from all the parishioners but the lairds and heritors paid the lion's share. The Lairds of Leckie, Gargunnock and Boquhan all contributed 300 merks. The small Lairds, Robert Stewart of Culbeg and James Forrester of Culmore, paid 100 merks each. When the bills for the rebuilding were presented in 1629, the Kirk Session discovered that there had been a 200 merk over-spend. Additional work inside the Kirk, a loft and some common forms were yet to be added, taking the overspend to 250 merks.[20]

A compulsory levy on all the parishioners to raise the outstanding sum was initially to be the answer. However, the minister was dissuaded, being told that the people would give more freely without compulsion. This was not a good idea. Two years later, during a Presbytery inspection, the books were checked and the overspend discovered. To add to the problem it was found that the Session had been raiding the Poor Fund to pay the interest on the 250 merks. The Presbytery ordered that all tenants in the parish be stented *pro rata* for the immediate payment of the outstanding amount.[21] The Minister should have known the building was going to be trouble when on the first day it was completely finished and newly glazed, bairns broke all the new windows. Two shillings per broken pane was to be paid by the parents or if they could not afford to pay, their masters or friends must do so.[22]

Also in 1631, John, Earl of Mar, who had gained possession of the church lands after the dissolution of Cambuskenneth Abbey in 1559, was asked to grant the area of an old wife's house and yard as an extension to the Kirk burial ground. The old woman's abode stood in the very bosom of the kirkyard. The request was granted and after the old woman died the area to the south of the kirk became a burial ground.[23] By way of thanks for their contributions towards the new building the Lairds were given their own seats in the Kirk and family burial plots in perpetuity. Over the next seventy years or so various modifications both inside and out, including lofts and stairs for the Lairds of Gargunnock, Leckie and Boquhan and a belfry built around 1702 on the northern gable, transformed the structure into the outlines of the present building.

The second rebuild was in 1774. The building had again fallen into decay and the Kirk was rebuilt. On the gables of the 1628 Kirk were two figures, a cross on the eastern and a crescent on the western, both were replaced on the new building.[24] There are a couple of explanations of the origins of the two signs, none of which is based on fact. One has it that they signify the rise of Christianity in the east and the demise of Islam in the west. Another is a remote, but considering the antiquity of the site, none too fanciful, connection with the Crusaders. Unfortunately, the rebuilding on both occasions was so complete that no vestiges of the earlier buildings remain.

Between the Reformation of the mid 16th century and the Revolution of 1688, Catholicism, Prelacy and Presbyterianism all vied for the souls of the parishioners. Each had periods of power which ushered in their own prejudices and acceptable codes of behaviour. Presbyterianism eventually gained the ascendancy and in 1690 became by constitution, the established church of the country. After the Reformation of 1560, there followed a long, bitter and at times very bloody series of conflicts about who controlled both the Kirk itself and to a degree the country.

The National Covenant of 1638, the Solemn League and Covenant of 1643 and involvement in the English Civil War, the Killing Times of 1660-90, when the Covenanters raised rebellion and took to the hills, were all periods of savage warfare which raged throughout the country and left few parishes completely unscathed.

Between 1639 and 1652 the parishioners of Gargunnock would have been living their lives under the cloud of civil war. The Parish Minister and the Kirk session were responsible for listing and fulfilling the quota of the fencible men (recruits) for the various armies of the Covenant, which was to be levied from the parish. The Minister and local lairds played a vital roll in encouraging eligible men to volunteer for the various Covenanting armies of the times. Additionally, the parishioners would have to support regiments or troops of soldiers which were quartered in the parish while mustering at or passing through Stirling. One such occasion was on 11th September 1648, when the Marquis of Argyll and 700 men, including 300 Campbell clansmen, arrived in Gargunnock from Dumbarton. The force spent the day in Gargunnock before marching on Stirling on the morning of 12th and capturing the town.[25]

Archibald Marquis of Argyll.

On occasion the parishioners were asked for additional contributions. In January 1645 a special donation of 18 pounds Scots was raised from the parishioners of Gargunnock to assist soldiers from the parish who were fighting with the Scots army in England against King Charles I. Another example was to raise ransom money to free some Christian slaves of the Turks. Yet another was the Irish Fund which was set up to help refugees from the marauding bands of Irish mercenaries who ravaged the west coast and particularly Argyll during the expeditions of Montrose and Alasdair MacColla.[26] Prior to their great victory at Kilsyth in the summer of 1645, the Earl of Montrose and his Irish allies crossed the Forth at the Ford of Frew and passed through the Parish en-route to Kilsyth. The news that the dreaded Irish were on their doorsteps would have spread terror among the good folk of Gargunnock, with most heading for the hills with their few possessions and livestock, Stirling and its castle being out of bounds due to the plague.[27]

The Kirk was, in the form of its Minister and Elders, at the very centre of the parishioners existence. The Parish Minister baptised their children, educated, married them and eventually buried them. As one of the few men in the Parish who was educated, the Minister mediated in disputes and advised his parishioners on most subjects. Vitally, he also had the ear of the Laird. Just about every facet of their lives had some link back to the Kirk and the Parish. In September 1651 the parish lost one of its longest serving Ministers when Reverend William Justice M.A. died. He arrived in the parish in 1615 and was its first recorded Minister.[28]

In October 1652, a new Minister called Archibald Muschet arrived in the parish. An entry in the Session records for December 1652 states *'that although the new minister is not yet settled in the manse, he intends to visit all his parishioners in their homes at the earliest opportunity'*. It was at this time, November 1652, that the Kirk Session, perhaps at the suggestion of the new minister, decided that they wanted a constant (permanent) school. Although there was a school and a paid schoolmaster called

Andrew Chamber at the Kirk as early as 1631, it was apparently a part-time affair. By 1652 the schoolmaster was a Mr Alexander Ronald who had been keeping school at Gargunnock for two years. He had been found to be diligent and was therefore offered the permanent position of Schoolmaster and Precentor at a salary of four score (80) merks, plus a suit of clothes per annum, first payment to be at Martinmas (11 November) 1653. The Elders were instructed to go through their divisions ensuring all children attended school and to note those parents who kept their children at home.[29] The Reverend Mr Muschet remained in the parish until 1662 when he was transferred to Larbert. Thirty odd years later the Education Act of 1696 instructed that there should be a school in every parish, the heritors of the parish were to provide a commodious house for a school and the schoolmaster's salary was not be less than 100 merks (£5.11s 1d) or more than 200 merks per year. The Gargunnock schoolmaster had complained in 1654 that despite all their promises nothing had been done by the heritors regarding his salary.[30] Possibly, the schoolmaster's salary had been raised in the interim, but if not, this was a long overdue pay rise.

Education was not free and pupils paid, usually quarterly, for their lessons. The fees of children of poor parents might be paid by the Kirk Session or by endowments for the purpose of education. Ideally children would remain at school until they were 12 or 13, but often the schooling, which was not compulsory, was sporadic and interrupted by the death or resignation of the teacher, who was not so easily replaced. The children of poor parents suffered most disruption having both to help more regularly at home and to leave school earlier to contribute fully to the family income. The busiest times in the agricultural year would see school attendance plummet as reading and writing took second place to sowing or harvest.[31] Lessons in the parish school included reading (usually the scriptures), writing, arithmetic and perhaps Latin. When Gargunnock Parish School opened in 1653 the lessons were initially conducted at the Kirk. However, in January 1654 it was decided that the school should be nearer the middle of the parish at a place called the Trolling or Trotting Ford.[32] The decision was obviously a contentious one and required some debate. In January 1656 after a vote, it was decided to move the school to a building at the Burn of Leckie. The tenants of both Meiklewood and Gargunnock protested but the motion was carried.[33] The parish school eventually returned to Gargunnock, but the exact date of the move back is not known. It was possibly when the school mentioned in the Old Statistical Account was built in 1789. As a concession to the scholars of Leckie and Boquhan, it was sited towards the western edge of Gargunnock Barony, outside the village boundary of the time, but fairly central to the parish.[34]

Early Presbyterianism with its strict Calvinist doctrine was a dour, joyless, stark religion of predestination of the damned and the righteous. The Kirk Elders who made up the Kirk Session were effectively a civil and moral court, who ensured the parishioners adhered to a long list of Do's and Don'ts, issued by the Assemblies, Synods, and Presbyteries. Many of the moral misdemeanours were also made statutory offences; adultery in 1563, Sabbath-breaking in 1579, drunkenness in 1617. In 1643 and 1645 respectively, scandalous behaviour at wakes and wedding ceremonies called Penny Bridals came to the notice of the great and the good of the General Assembly. In the case of the former it was ordained that none should come to the house of the deceased apart from six or seven close friends invited to comfort the relatives and they must leave before 10 at night.[35] In the case of the latter, it was felt that there was too much fun being had at Penny Bridals by the multitude attending, with the lascivious carriage of men and women, by

GARGUNNOCK KIRK – This building is at least the third Church on the site. It was originally a rectangular building built in 1774, the cross which was removed from the previous structure built in 1628, can just be seen on top of the eastern gable. The northern extension with its bell tower and both sets of stairs are later additions.

promiscuous dancing and pipers playing. In future the bride and groom were only to have three or four guests at the most and there were to be no pipers and no dancing.[36]

All these misdemeanours attracted some form of retribution usually in the form of a fine and or public humiliation, the latter perhaps requiring a number of appearances on the stool of repentance, before the entire congregation. The stool took various forms but most were a raised platform on which the miscreants stood while the Minister pointed out the error of their ways and held them up as an example to the assembled congregation. The person was usually then required to seek the forgiveness of his neighbours for his or her failing. If additional humiliation was required the offender could be required to wear haircloth or white sheeting. Until the end of the 17th century punishments could be much more severe and there is evidence of such in Gargunnock. There were a number of cases of persistent offenders being locked by the neck, bare footed in the Kirk *'jougs'* for periods of up to six days. The joug was a lockable metal collar linked to a chain which was either attached to the outside Kirk wall or to a post positioned where most people could see the offender. While in the jougs the unfortunates would be given little or nothing to eat while they pondered on their misdeeds.

Punishments usually included fines, the Kirk being always ready to take wrong-doers' money to assist with charitable causes. In Gargunnock Parish in the Year of Our Lord 1625, being found drinking on the Sabbath would cost 6s. 8d, from both the giver and the receiver, plus public repentance. Working on the Sabbath, like cutting peat or bleaching cloth, cost 13s 4d. For the first fornication offence it was 2 merks and three Sundays on the stool. A second fornication offence cost 4 merks and six days on the stool in haircloth or white sheeting. If you could not pay you went into the jougs. For adultery it was 10 merks and straight into the Jougs for six days, bare footed and bare headed.[37] During the 17th century a Pound Scots was worth one twelfth of the Pound Sterling or 1/8d (8½ p).[38]

More serious offences could, if the initial Session investigation thought it necessary, be sent up to the next higher church authority at the Presbytery or even beyond. The most serious cases in the Parish in the 1620s and 30s were two cases of witchcraft. The first was investigated by the Gargunnock Kirk Session beginning on 12th May 1626. Janet Lochart, spouse of James Miller in Leckie, was accused of seeking her cow's milk on her knees from earthly and unearthly creatures as told to do by a neighbour Steven Maltman. She alleged that Maltman had taken her cow's milk by witchcraft and when approached, he advised her to use witchcraft to get it back. The Session decided that the case was too hot for them to handle and sent it up to the Presbytery.[39]

Another case of witchcraft in Gargunnock came to light in July 1631. This time the woman, Marjory Kerr, took the advice of a neighbour Rosie Graham on an unusual cure for her sick cow. The woman was to get from a neighbour a cat without asking for it by name. She was to take the cat to the cow and pass it under the cow three times, then throw the poor cat out the door. She had then to take off her left shoe and again pass it under the cow three times, slapping the cow with the sole of the shoe each time. She then had to take milk from the cow and put it into a hole in a place which got no light. Afterwards she was to mix it with water from the boundary or March burn and pour the mixture thrice into the cow's lug, all which she confessed she did, getting the cat from the house of William Swan.

The Session decided that the matter was odious and uncouth and since the Presbytery was due to visit, the matter would be referred to them. In the case of Marjory Kerr the Presbytery decided she was just a foolish woman, but she had to make her public repentance upon the public place in her linings and to be punished in her goods and gear at the sight of the Session who knew her estate. Both Janet Lochart and Steven Maltman were tried by the Presbytery, the outcome is unfortunately unknown. Perhaps there was something in the old remedies for according to Marjory Kerr, her cow was just great after its unusual cure.[40]

These people were extremely fortunate that the Stirling baillies and their Presbytery took a more enlightened view of witchcraft than some others. Those involved were literally playing with fire, suspected witches were still regularly being tortured and burned at the stake, usually along with a number of their neighbours whom they had implicated in the affair. The bailies and the Presbytery had the power to banish offenders from the parish. Excommunication from the Church meant the person was also an outlaw from civil society. They could not hold any office or lands or receive rents. This was a very serious matter for the individual concerned. Without a testificate or reference from the parish, he or she would find it difficult if not impossible to settle elsewhere in Scotland as no parish would accept them without the testificate. In all probability he or she would end up as a wandering vagrant, begging to stay alive. It would appear that many of the old superstitions were alive and well in Gargunnock parish in the early 17th century. In May 1626 a general instruction was made to all parishioners to the effect that they were to cease going to Christie's Well for cures for illnesses. Anyone found to be adhering to the superstition would be fined 40s and be put into white sheets.[41]

The two jewels in the crown of the early kirk were its commitment to education which we have already looked at and the Poor Fund, a form of social security for the infirm poor of the parish. A parliamentary act of 1579 made the parish responsible by law for the care of the poor. It stated that the infirm, but not the able bodied, were entitled to poor relief. The administration of the relief was carried out by the individual Kirk Sessions and would take the form of small cash payments or the provision of food or quantities of coal or peat. The fund was maintained by voluntary contributions, collections at the Kirk door, baptism and marriage fees, donations and gifts from wealthy parishioners and by hiring out mortcloths for funerals. The mortcloth was usually black satin or velvet and covered the coffin en-route to the grave. The first Parish mortcloth was bought in 1659 and cost £42.13s 4d (Scots).[42] Before a person could receive relief in Gargunnock, they must have resided in the parish for at least three years and had to apply for support. The case was then looked at by the Session and the need of the applicant investigated.[43] There were exceptions to the rule and during the religious wars of the mid 17th century refugees from the troubles in Ireland and Argyll were often given immediate relief.[44]

Agnes Smith of Gargunnock made the first recorded application for a pension from the Parish in February 1626. She applied for relief on account of her age and infirmities and after due consideration was awarded 10s to be paid quarterly.[45] A hundred and seventy years later in 1796, depending on the degree of want, the successful applicant could receive between 2s 6d (12.5p) to 10s (50p) per month. Gargunnock Parish Poor Fund was sufficiently well endowed to provide supplies of meal and coal, particularly during the winter months, to those parishioners who had not applied for relief, but whom the Session considered to be in some need.

No public begging was allowed and in 1796, the sixteen parishioners receiving funds at the time were only 2% of the Parish population.[46] Gargunnock Parish considered itself among the best in Scotland, regarding the provision it gave to its widows, fatherless, aged and infirm. Unfortunately, then as today, there were people who would abuse or take advantage of the system. Just such a case came to light in Gargunnock in the year 1784.

Two old sisters who lived in Gargunnock village gave the impression of poverty for many years, though neither had applied to the parish for assistance. At last one sister applied and was accepted on to the parish poor list without question, receiving four shillings per month as a pension. Six months after receiving the pension the old woman died. Poor Fund rules decreed that the property of those who died while receiving money from the poor fund belonged to the parish. Soon after the old woman died, members of the session arrived at her house to go through her possessions. They discovered purse after purse stuffed with gold and silver coins worth £40.00. Additionally, the house was full of barrels of cheese, beef, meal and various other foodstuffs. Far from being in poverty the old sisters lived in some luxury. When the relations of the old woman heard of the discovery they arrived to claim their inheritance. They were informed that the parish claimed half the find as was their right, the other half was given to the second sister who had not claimed on the fund. The relations received nothing which was generally regarded as their just reward since they took little heed of the old woman while she lived. The parish funds were the best part of £20 richer for the incident.[47]

The registers of Gargunnock Parish go back to 1615 with the arrival of the first recorded Minister, Mr William Justice, born about 1590. Unfortunately, there are large gaps in the registers, particularly the last forty years of the 17th century. The very early Ministers of Gargunnock were an interesting lot. Two of the most so were Mr John Edmondstone, born in 1630 the son of Mr James Edmondstone, Minister of nearby St Ninians parish. Educated at the University of St Andrews he arrived as Minister of Gargunnock in September 1666. Twice married, he was deprived of his parish in 1689 for his immoderate drinking and other undisclosed scandalous practices. The heritors of the parish had previously been ordered by the Privy Council to pay him 6000 merks in compensation for his parishioners rioting against him and his family.[48] Another, Mr George Barcley, was a covenanter and was arrested and confined in the guardhouse in Edinburgh in 1679, probably for unlawful preaching. He managed to escape by leaping through a window and made his way through England to Holland. He returned in 1685 and preached at conventicles in Galloway and Ayrshire. He was the Minister at a meeting house in Gargunnock Parish between 1688 and 1690.[49]

Into the 18th Century

The 17th century ended with more upheaval and deaths as the Stewart dynasty and the harvests between 1695 and 1699 failed. The Glorious Revolution of 1688 saw the Catholic James VII deposed and the thrones of Scotland and England offered to William of Orange and his wife Mary Stuart. The famine years were known as King William's Ill Years, the horror of which was seared into the minds of the survivors. The food shortages were on a similar scale to the Irish Potato famine of the 1840s. Some estimates put the death and emigration rate in some parishes as high as a third to a half. One fifth of the entire Scottish nation (200,000) was on the road looking for food.[50] Horror stories of people eating grass and of others crawling towards kirkyards in order to be given a Christian burial abound. Unlike previous famines it was not the most vulnerable such as the very poor, the old and the children who were dying. This famine affected just about everyone. The vast majority of people, even those living in the towns, still depended on farming to live, they grew what they ate. If nothing grew they had nothing to eat. They might be able to scrape through one or two bad harvests, but once they had to eat their seed crop there was nothing left to plant.

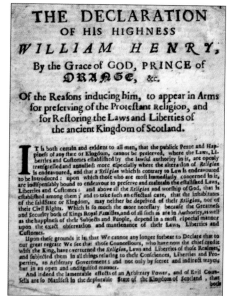

Propaganda supporting the Glorious Revolution.

In Gargunnock the effects would have been just as bad. It was food itself which was scarce and even if you had money, in many places it simply could not be bought. Stirling Burgh records state that in 1695 they were turning away daily 80 vagrants from outwith the town and helping 150 others at the Kirk of the Holy Rude.[51] It was said of the time that *"the living were too weak to bury the dead"*.

By the beginning of the century, Scotland as a nation was impoverished. Decades of religious strife had exacerbated the problems of an already desperately poor country. The ill-fated Darien adventure of 1698 had stripped all levels of society of a large portion of what little cash money there was in the country. The attempt to establish a Scottish colony, (Darien), on the Panama isthmus, in which everyone from the highest to the lowest in Scottish society invested what little quantities of cash they had, failed disastrously, mainly through English protectionism, Spanish attacks and local tropical diseases, not to mention a large degree of Scottish mismanagement. The poor state of the nation added weight to the political arguments of those Scots who wished for reasons sometimes other than patriotism, to unite the country with England. The Scottish and English crowns had been united since James VI of Scotland succeeded Elizabeth I of England in 1603. For centuries the English had tried to subjugate the Scots by force of arms and had failed. Now, with the collusion of some Scots nobles, political intrigue and economic shenanigans they had succeeded where force had failed. On 1st May 1707, political union with England came into force. The bells of St. Giles in Edinburgh, played the tune *Why should I be sad on my wedding day?*

The union brought few immediate benefits to the country and initially, the exact opposite was true as political power moved south to London and costlier English taxes moved north to Scotland. Generally, Scottish traders were ill equipped to compete with their English counterparts under the new conditions of free trade. The Union of Parliaments did bring two major benefits, both of which were fairly quickly apparent. Firstly, English markets opened up to Scottish exports particularly cattle, and secondly, fresh modern ideas particularly in agriculture began to be introduced into Scotland, as politicians and landowners travelling through England saw how backward Scotland really was. The great famine and the Union were both to prove watersheds and the beginnings of an enormous effort to improve and modernise which would eventually transform the entire country.

Politically, the first 50 years of the 18th century saw the Union of the Scottish and English Parliaments, two major rebellions and a number of significant laws enacted which changed lifestyles and customs which had been in place for hundreds of years. Although the Glorious Revolution of 1688 was for the most part bloodless and welcomed in most quarters, in Scotland particularly, the political union with the auld enemy was not so warmly welcomed and in its first years soured even further, with riots in Glasgow and Edinburgh. The first Jacobite rebellion of 1715 saw the major landowner in Gargunnock Parish, John Earl of Mar, Lord Erskine, raise the Stewart King's standard on the Braes of Mar. Bobbing Johnny, as he was known, was destined to loose all his lands and possessions after the rebellion failed, in part, due to his own indecisiveness. He later died disillusioned and penniless in France.

The Arms of Campbell of Ardkinlass.

A portion of the Earl of Mar's Gargunnock lands had been feued to James Campbell of Ardkinlass in 1707 and was included in his forfeited estates. Ardkinlass was required to plead his cause to the Lords of Session, his argument being that since he had remained loyal to the king, he should be allowed to retain possession of the Gargunnock lands, irrespective of his former feudal superior's treacherous behaviour. The Lords of Session agreed and in 1719, allowed him to retain his lands, while the remainder of Mar estate was sold. Ardkinlass now held his lands directly from the Crown itself. Included in the document confirming this decision is a list of the lands within the barony which now belonged to Ardkinlass. In addition to the 20 merk lands of old extent (about 1200 acres), they included the Kirk or Chapel lands, Flechams, one third of Meiklewood and interestingly the Kirktoun of Gargunnock.[52] Much of the terminology in these old legal documents is taken directly from earlier charters which are always very accurate and precise when detailing the ownership of land. This last reference to a Kirktoun of Gargunnock suggests an earlier settlement, perhaps late medieval, based around the old Roman Catholic Chapel of pre-reformation times. The location nearby of Gargunnock Mill also suggests a substantial community in the neighbourhood of the present village, certainly more than the three or four poor houses of the 1720s, mentioned in the first Statistical Account. The earlier reference to Gargunnock Kirkyerd of 1630 being extended once they had removed an old woman's house, also lends credence to the supposition.

There is no physical reason why the area around the kirk and mill could not maintain a sizeable toun, both establishments being recognised nuclei for settlements. The disappearance or decay of the kirktoun could be explained by a number of factors. Touns often moved or split or as the land became exhausted. Hence the profusion of Upper or Lower or East or West or Over and Under seen even on modern maps. The Reformation saw the redistribution of massive amounts of church land, with most going to powerful nobles. In Gargunnock's case, the Earl of Mar got the lion's share of the chapel lands and he may or may not have supported the new Kirk. Although enthusiastic about the opportunity to join in the feeding frenzy over the vast church lands, the conduct by the Mar family 50 years later shows at least Episcopalian, if not Catholic, leanings. There may have been a period between the abandonment of the old Roman Chapel and the establishment of the new Protestant Kirk, where the religious organisation which

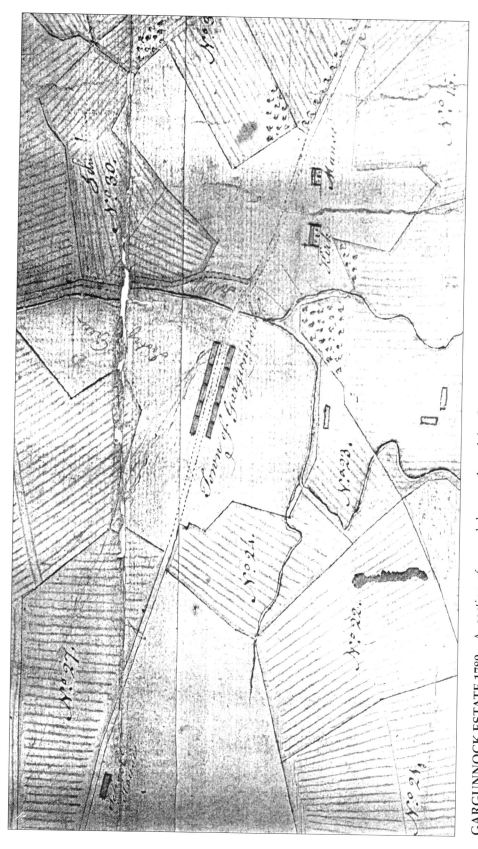

GARGUNNOCK ESTATE 1789 – A section of a much larger plan of the Gargunnock Estate in 1789. It shows clearly the lineal development of the village along the military road which at that time still ran through the village. The area around the square is shown as undeveloped, in 1789 this area still belonged to the Gourleys' of Kipdarroch and was not acquired by Eidingtoun of Gargunnock until the mid 1790s. Also seen to the west is the newly built Parish Schoolhouse. Its location was a probably a concession to the scholars of Leckie and Boquhan.

perhaps had held the settlement together was abandoned. The Kirk of Gargunnock as a pendicle of St Ninian's, is mentioned in an Act of the old Scots Parliament of 1606.[53] However, the parish registers only begin in 1615 and this may be some indication of the re-establishment of religious worship on the site.

Between the rebellions of 1715 and 1745, the deposed Stewart monarchy in exile in France continued to plot and foster the resentment and unrest. Meanwhile, Scotland as a whole slowly began to feel the benefits of the union with England, which in part helped to ensured the failure of the second rebellion. These years saw the acceleration of change in almost every facet of Scottish life. In 1723, a society of agricultural improvers was founded, as was the merchant bank of John Coutts in Edinburgh. The following year General Wade was appointed Commander in Chief in Scotland, he would subsequently lay hundreds of miles of good roads and build over 40 bridges throughout the Highlands. The same year John Cockburn was experimenting with potatoes. In 1727, the Board of Commissioners for Manufactures was appointed. This helped to protect and nurture the Scottish Linen trade. The Royal Bank of Scotland was founded and Janet Horne a reputed witch was the last to be burned in Scotland. In 1733, as a sign of a more moderate Kirk, a theatre was opened in Edinburgh. Linen manufacture, cotton weaving and iron working were introduced or expanded, but nowhere was the change more pronounced than in agriculture. After the Forty Five, Great Britain embarked on a series of international conflicts, mostly with France, which were to last until the final defeat of Napoleon at Waterloo and helped fuel 50 boom years.

For most of the 18th century the majority of people in the parish were still living in fermtouns and small individual farms. The sweeping agricultural improvements of the first half of the 18th century saw the destruction of the old farmtoun communities, the second half the century saw the start of a process of consolidating the smaller farms into single occupancy larger farms. Firstly the fermtoun folk, then later the small tenant farmer and his cotters were forced into the village to work as landless agricultural labourers on the new larger farms or move out of the parish to the various towns along the Clyde valley, which were rapidly becoming industrialised. The process of consolidation would continue well into the 19th century. The present village of Gargunnock is a fairly recent development and was in fact an experiment in social engineering. According to the Old Statistical Account, as late as the 1720s, there was only a collection of three or four poorly built houses in the area. Sixty or so years later there were still people alive who remembered it as such.[54] This statement refers to the area on which the new, then, Gargunnock village developed and does not mean that the area was previously uninhabited. There is some evidence which we shall look at later which suggests that there were substantial settlements around the area of the Kirk and nearby Courthill.

Between 1726 and the 1780s, Gargunnock village itself was established and grew to about 400 people, mostly agricultural labourers, but also with weavers, masons, wrights, a tailor, and a couple of shoemakers.[55] Feus on which people could build houses were made available mostly in half and quarter acre plots in two main phases. The first was for the lower end of the village between 1726 and 1733.[56] The feus were for land on both sides of the old road, beginning next to the bridge. Each new feu took the plots further up the hill towards Leckie, particularly on the north of the road. The second phase was for the upper part of the village on the southern side of the road, beginning in 1772.[57] Although there were only about

The Pack Horse Bridge at Leckie Mill

A view of the old Pack Horse bridge at the Mill of Leckie. It was built in 1673 to span the Leckie Burn on the old Stirling to Dumbarton road. It bears the following inscription on the parapet, *Ex Benevolentia ob salutem* (literally, (built) out of good will for safety).

27 feus in the village, most were sublet and subdivided to allow others to build houses. By 1790, the village consisted of about 90 houses, chiefly of one floor with thatched and later tile roofs. The houses would usually consist of two rooms, one for living in, the other being used as a workroom or perhaps let to lodgers. Each of the original feus also possessed a long narrow plot of land. These were split into yards or gardens in which the feuar and his tenants could grow an assortment of garden crops and perhaps keep the odd cow.[58]

Until the middle of the 18th century roads of any quality were non existent in Scotland. The route between two of Scotland's most important castles Stirling and Dumbarton, lay through the parish and until the mid 1750s, was little more than a medieval track. It probably followed an even earlier path which took the easiest route for a man on foot or a pack animal between the edge of the boggy carse lands and the slope of the dryfields. About 1755 the dirt track was upgraded by the Hanoverian road builders who required good military communications between Stirling and Dumbarton. It would appear that the new military road followed the route of the old track for at least part of its length, particularly while passing through the parish and the expanding village which was then growing on both sides of the old track. The military road appears to have taken advantage of existing bridges, such as Gargunnock Bridge and a span near Leckie House. The exact date of the building of the first Gargunnock Bridge is unknown, however, there is a reference in the Kirk Session Minutes calling for a bridge to be built over the Gargunnock Burn, dated March 1655. Unfortunately, there is no mention of the bridge actually being built.[59] There would undoubtedly have been some form of bridge, (albeit large stepping stones) crossing the Gargunnock Burn in the area of the present bridge since the very earliest times. The span at Leckie is a fine stone packhorse bridge adjacent to the old mill of Leckie and has a stone recording the date 1673 and the Latin text *Ex Benevolentia ob Salutem* (literally, out of good will for safety).[60]

Some time between 1792 and 1796 this military road was upgraded to a turnpike road. This relieved the parishioners of the burden of statute labour, which saw them having to give a certain number of days labour maintaining the road. At the same time a new bridge was built 15 metres to the north of the old bridge.[61] This span carried the new road around the hill feature on the slope of which Gargunnock village stands. The diversion was probably in response to the expected increased volume of horse-drawn coaches and carts which would have found the steep gradient through the village heavy going.

The Moir of Leckie crest.

In the late 1790s, when the history of the house begins, the major land owners and heritors of the parish were, Charles Alexander Moir, Esq. of Leckie, Colonel James Eidingtoun of Gargunnock, Mr Graham of Meiklewood and Henry Fletcher Campbell Esq. of Boquhan. These four were the Feudal Superiors or Tenants in Chief of the lands in the parish.[62] The main estates in the parish were therefore Gargunnock, Meiklewood, Leckie and Boquhan.

The Moir family gained the Leckie estate in 1668. David Moir of Craigarnhall was the lawyer of the last of the Leckies of Leckie. The then laird, John Leckie, borrowed money from Moir secured on the Leckie estate. In 1668

Old Gargunnock House

There has been a fortified building on the site of Gargunnock House since at least the late 15th century. In 1513, Ninian Seyton, son of Alexander Seyton, paid entry money to the King for a sixth part of the lands of Gargunnock" with the tower, fortalice and mansion of the same." The crow step gable and single turret are typical of the period.

the estate was transferred to Moir in payment of the loan thus ending the Leckie family connection which had lasted over 300 years.[63] Dr Charles Graham Moir succeeded to the property in June 1820 and built the new mansion house of Leckie. The Moirs would remain at Leckie until the beginning of the 20th century when the estate was sold by Alastair Graham Moir to Mr George Younger of Valleyfield, Kinross in 1906.

The feus for the barony of Gargunnock had only recently been aquired by Col James Eidingtoun of Gargunnock (1793). For almost a century before, the Barony of Gargunnock was in the possession of a family of Campbells of Ardkinlass.[64] By the mid 1830s, Charles Stirling, 5th son of John Stirling of Kippendavie, was the proprietor having bought the feus from the trustees of the of Eidington estate. The Stirlings of Gargunnock would remain as Feudal Superiors until 1989 when the last of the line, Miss Viola H. Stirling CBE, died.

The ancestors of the Grahams of Meiklewood had been in the parish since in 15th century. One, David Graham of Gargunnock, had disputed the title of the Gargunnock lands with the Normanvil family in 1470. The Grahams had been on their Meiklewood lands since the 16th century having married into the family of Lord Elphinstone then proprietor in 1581. In 1679, the Grahams of Meiklewood also gained the lands and toun of Courthill to the east of the Kirk of Gargunnock.[65]

On the western side of the parish the lands of Boquhan had been for many years in the possession of a cadet branch of the Campbells of Argyll. In 1690, the then Laird, James Campbell of Burnbank and Boquhan, 4th son of Archibald the 9th Earl of Argyll, with the aid of two accomplices, forcibly carried off and married Mary, 13-year-old daughter and heiress of Sir George Wharton. The marriage was annulled by an act of parliament and one of the accomplices, Sir John Johnston, was executed at Tyburn. James Campbell escaped back to Scotland where afterward he became a colonel of dragoons and MP for Renfrew between 1699 and 1707. The property came to the Fletcher Campbells through Mary, daughter of Colonel James Campbell of Burnbank and Boquhan, who left the lands to her cousin General Henry Fletcher of Saltoun.[66]

The Seton lands of Touch lay on the eastern border of the parish and although just outside the boundary, ally themselves more to Gargunnock than to their own St Ninian's parish. The Seton family first came into possession of their lands of Touch in 1449 through the marriage of Sir Alexander Seton, Earl of Huntly and Egidia, daughter of John Hay of Tullibody. The Hays had previously inherited Touch from the Frasers. The Setons once possessed a large portion of Gargunnock, including the fortalice and manor before disposing of them to the Earl of Mar.[67] The Seton descendants remained at Touch until the 1920s when the property was sold to a family of Buchanans.

Little more information on the major landed families of the parish has been included in this narrative, other than when it has a direct and obvious bearing on the particular point being covered at the time. The histories and genealogies of the landed families have been well documented and are readily available for those with such an interest.

James McNair's Feu

In the name of God Amen. Know ye all men by this present public instrument that upon the tenth day of January Seventeen Hundred and Ninety Six years and of the reign of our sovereign Lord, George the Third by the grace of God of Great Britain, France and Ireland King, defender of the faith, his thirty seventh year.

So begins the instrument of sasine dated 1796 in which John Murdoch Jnr, from nearby Beild of Leckie, officially took possession of the grounds on which he built the dwelling house, which was still known as late as the 1960s as the Guest House and is now called Trelawney Cottage.[68] The building has overlooked the Square in Gargunnock, for around 200 years. In fact, the sasine of 1796 is not the earliest specific record of the grounds. A generation earlier the feu was bought by Mr James McNair, a 26 year old tailor in Gargunnock, from Mr David Gourley of Kippdarroch, on 26th November 1777. On the sasine of that date, the property is described as

> 'All and Whole that House and Yeard (garden enclosure) with trees lying in the village of Gargunnock, and also all and whole that small enclosure or small piece of ground separated from the said house by the King's highway and part of Gargunnock Bridge'.[69]

It is not known for how long David Gourley owned the property, but we do know that he bought it from a Mr Archibald Abercromby, who was a cooper or barrel maker. The dimensions of the feu mentioned in the document of 1777 correspond to a roughly triangular area, between Leckie Road as it crosses the Square in front of the terrace and the Gargunnock stream and the road from the Square to the main Dumbarton/Stirling road. The base of the triangle being the main road along the front of the terrace with the apex to the north, where the stream and the road to the main Dumbarton/Stirling road meet just before Waterside house. The feu therefore included the land on which the houses and gardens of McNair House, Glenfoyle Cottage (once part of McNair House), Trelawney Cottage and the new Waterside House (built in the 1960s) to the north. Also included in the original feu was that piece of ground now on the south side of Leckie road, which the Stevenson Memorial fountain and Garden now occupy. James McNair also possessed the feu for the properties on the south side of the Square, including that on which the old Free Kirk School once stood. *(See feu map at appendix VII).*

In the mid 18th century land was still regarded as the basis of all power. The nobility and major landowners assessed their wealth in acres and the strength of their tails, as opposed to cash. However, the winds of change were blowing and this system was beginning to break down. James McNair was a feuar and owned the land under a system known as Feuferme. The advantage of a feu over a tenancy was security of tenure. The feu allowed heritable possession, therefore the property could be passed from father to son down the generations and encouraged the feu holder to improve the property. A feu was gained from the landowner by paying him a large sum of cash known as a *'Grassum'*. Cash money was still in relatively short supply and generally only lairds or in-comers like lawyers or businessmen could afford the large amounts required to buy a substantial feu.

No evidence has yet been found to suggest where James McNair found the money, though we know he was a tailor to trade and may therefore have been able to amass the cash required. Often these small tradesmen like tailors were also moneylenders. This was simply because they were some of the few people who handled and dealt in cash, though they would undoubtably have accepted the odd chicken or half dozen eggs in payment. The grassum was followed yearly by a fixed sum called Feu-Duty. These sums were fixed in perpetuity and the value decreased in real terms as the years passed, so that the feuar kept more of his labours and so theoretically prospered. The annual feu-duty could be paid partly in cash and party in kind. Various measures of grain, animals or labour for the feudal superior made up the payment. Church stipends (payments to the local parish church, usually to assist with the minister's salary) and the requirement to have any grain produced ground at a certain mill, usually the feudal superior's, for a percentage of the whole was generally included in the feu contract.

The system of payment to the miller was known as *"Thirlage"*. The payment was called *"Multure"* and had to be paid whether the grain was ground at the mill or not. Thirlage was very unpopular with everyone, for most people grew some crops, but with the farmers especially, for obvious reasons. The fraction due to the miller was usually around an eleventh of the grain ground. Despite its unpopularity, thirlage remained in force until 1777, when an Act of Parliament replaced it with cash terms. However, in the feu contract between James McNair and David Gourley of November 1777, the thirlage clause is still included. The inclusion is there more for custom, as the acreage involved in the feu was too small to make a great difference to James McNair.

'James McNair is to carry his grindable grain seed , horse corn excepted, to the mill of Gargunnock to be grind and pay multures and dues therefore accustomed and to perform due services to the mill and dams thereof used and wont'.

Mr James Robertson in his statistical account of 1794 comments on the feudal system as it comes under increasing pressure to modernise. He mentions the old thirlage and multure system and comments,

'the farmers justly complained about the tax, now they cheerfully pay one shilling per acre to the miller to defray his necessary expenses'.

Also on the feu duties payable, he suggests

'the variety of services due, fowls, to drive coals, peat and dung. At harvest, time to cut the proprietor's grain, are all a great inconvenience, leaving the tenant unable to concentrate on his own business, sometimes missing opportunities which can never be regained'.

Another burden assigned to the feuar was the responsibility of contributing towards the Minister's stipend and if the village had one, the teacher's salary. In James McNair's case he was burdened with both, to the tune of two pounds per year. As his annual feu duty was two pounds five shillings, due at Martinmas (11 November), his yearly expenses as far as the property was concerned, was therefore four pounds five shillings sterling, not forgetting the six chickens payable at Lammas (1st August). Unfortunately, there was no mention of how much the initial payment or grassum cost. An additional burden on this particular property was the surrender of six months worth of *"Saugh"* which was the name for willow withes from which willow ropes were once made. The ropes were used to tie down turf or broom roof coverings on the old houses. The trees mentioned in the feu contract were obviously willows.[70]

James McNair gained his feu at a time of great change both locally and in the country as a whole. By the 1770s, Scotland was in the midst of an enormous effort to change a backward, barely productive agricultural industry into something which could both support the increasing population and produce profit for the landowners and those who worked the land for them. The landscape of Scotland at the time was unlike that which we see today. For the most part the land was open rough country, with no hedges or stone walls other than those around the houses and gardens of the gentry. There were few trees and roads as we know them were non-existent. Large areas of the country were unsuitable for cultivation being too hilly or moorland or peatbog. In a country as wet as Scotland, even the best land could be wet, boggy and difficult to drain.

The Carse of Kincardine which stretched along the northern edge of the parish was typical. Even today we can see how quickly the reclaimed farmland becomes water-logged. Any journeys out of the district were only undertaken when absolutely necessary and were conducted either on horseback or on foot. The little amount of goods that moved across the country was transported on pack animals or on sledges dragged by horses. In winter, movement became almost impossible, as the few dirt tracks there were turned into quagmires. Snow when it fell lay for much longer than it does today, simply because people had to wait until it thawed, rather than have it cleared for them. Gargunnock of course, had the advantage of sitting astride the major road or track between Stirling and Dumbarton, which should have cleared quicker than most.

The vast majority of Scots, estimated to be around one million, lived in the countryside and depended on agriculture for their livelihoods. Scottish agriculture had changed very little since medieval times and the preoccupation of most people was simply the production of enough food to stave off starvation. Famines often ravaged the country or parts of it, as weak crops fell prey to the least fluctuation in the weather. The lack of reliable communications and an adequate transportation system meant that one part of the country could be in famine while another had plenty. Although by the middle of the 18th century famines on the scale of King *William's Ill Years* were thankfully things of the past, serious local food shortages still often occurred. The worse effects of the shortages were avoided thanks to improved communications which gave information of the shortages, thereby allowing imported grain to arrive from other parts of the country in time. Both James McNair and David Gourley would have remembered local food shortages.

18th Century Living Conditions

At the beginning of the 18th century most country folk, and that was the majority of the population, were small farmers and the fermtoun people. They lived in very basic one room cottages, the low walls of which would be constructed of undressed stone and turf clods. The roof would be thatched or covered with peat and inside there would be a packed earth floor. There would be no glass in the windows only wooden shutters, if there were window openings at all. The open fire was set on the floor in the centre of the room and some of the smoke would escape through a hole in the roof. The fire would be fuelled with peat or coal, the latter being found in great abundance in Bannockburn parish.[71]

Any animals the people owned would share the same roof, entering by the same door which was often belly deep in mud. Inside only a wooden partition might separate the animals from the people. Although unhygienic, the animals provided much needed warmth during the cold winter nights. The interiors would be gloomy if not dark with the only light coming from the fire or the odd home made candle. Human and animal waste was valuable and was used as fertiliser. Both would be saved on the family dunghill which was usually just outside the main entrance.[72] Beds would be no more than a pile of straw or heather and depending on their means, they may have owned a few wooden stools and a kist for their few possessions. Even fairly wealthy people owned remarkably little. The small farmer and his cotters owned almost nothing: a couple of wooden stools, a horn spoon and a knife, a few wooden bowls, some cooking utensils, some basic tools and perhaps a good blue bonnet kept especially for market day or Sundays. They drew water from a local well or stream, but seldom used this water as a drink. They generally drank home made ale and the occasional whisky at celebrations. It is difficult for us to imagine what it must have been like to live in these conditions, let alone bear and raise children.

What follows is a description of such a farming community from *Scottish Men of Letters of the Eighteenth Century* by Graham Gray

> *Farmers and workers were much about the same rank; indeed in the holdings or "mailings", most of the work was done by the tenant's family with the aid of one or two or three men and women who lived with them. They all met at the same board, sat together by the fireside at night, when the women spun the flax and the men shoed their brogues; and partook of the same food , out of the same bowl, which was rarely cleaned. Each man had his own horn spoon, which he kept by his side or in his bonnet, to sup the kail, porridge or sowans; while his fingers and teeth did duty for fork and knife on the rare occasion when they were called into requisition by the death of "crock ewe", the meat being cut off by the farmer's clasp knife. The houses inside and out were filthy, though the dirt of their homes, of their food, and of their persons did not distress them, except in the familiar disease which too often came over their bodies. 'They loved this state' it kept them warm; it saved them trouble; and it enshrined their tastes in their sayings "The mair dirt the less hurt", "the clattier (dirtier) the cosier". Their exposure to all weathers outside and then to peat reek inside, which filled the room with smoke and feathered the rafters with soot, made their skins hard, brown, and withered, and old looking before their time.'*

The small farmer cultivating 20 or 30 acres would sublet a small piece of ground for a garden (kailyard) and few feet to build a cottage to one or two agricultural labourers called cotters, this in return for their labour around the farm. A collection of cottages may have clustered around a mill or a church and developed into a sizeable fermtoun or clachan as they were known in the Highlands. The fermtouns were collections of perhaps six to a dozen families perhaps interrelated, all working the land together, almost like a Jewish kibbutz. All had an interest in the land and everyone needed to work in co-operation with their neighbours to keep their land in cultivation. This highly communal system encouraged debate

Jean McAlpine's Inn

Although not in Gargunnock parish this photograph of Jean McAlpine's Inn near Aberfoyle, illustrates how bad the housing conditions could be. In fact this building appears to have been improved with what looks like a chimney on the far gable and window openings containing glass.

and agreed practices which over time became set in stone and resistant to change. Eventually, most working practices and decisions reached, took account of communal harmony as opposed to good working practices.

In traditional farming methods, the farm land was split into infield and outfield lands. The infield was closest to the fermtoun itself and being the best land it received all the available manure and was kept in continuous cultivation. The outfield was further away and was of lesser quality. It received little manure other than from grazing animals and was allowed to lie fallow to regain fertility after cultivation. The land was ploughed into long furrows called rigs which over the course of years became higher as the plough continuously turned the soil upwards in an attempt to drain it. Between the blocks of rigs were the baulks, strips of land which remained uncultivated and overgrown. This system of cultivation was known as *"Runrig"*. The ferm families would each be allocated a number of sections or strips of land in rotation, with each strip becoming of poorer quality. Every year the allocations would be rotated therefore ensuring the land was fairly distributed.

The plough in general use at the time is now known as the old Scots plough. This instrument was made almost entirely of wood, measured 13 feet in length and was very heavy. It required a minimum of four men to manage it, including one man who sat on the shear to keep the ploughhead in the ground and an oxen team of up to eight, yoked two by two, to propel it through the soil. Many of the old measurements seen in land documents refer to oxgangs, ploughgates and horse-gangs. These relate to areas which could be kept in cultivation by teams of animals.

The basic seed crops grown were bear or bere, which was a type of barley, and oats. A section of the infield lands was used to sow the bere. The seeds would be sown in the springtime and in a good year would produce a return of five grains for each one sown. Thereafter that section would be sown with oats until the land had recovered sufficiently to support another crop of bere. Oats were also sown on the poorer quality outfield lands but the returns would be generally poor. With the returns produced on each crop being so low, it takes little imagination to see how close to starvation levels most people lived. If a return of five seeds for every one planted was produced, two of them were required to pay the rent, one other was required for the next seed crop, which left only two to eat. If the yield fell below five to one, people would either go hungry or go into arrears with the rent. Two consecutive bad harvests could mean eating the next seed crop with obvious results. An old saying of the times sums up the situation well *'Ane tae saw, Ane tae gnaw an Ane tae pay the rent wie.'* (One to sow, one to grow and one to pay the rent with.)

In addition to the crops the people kept various animals, mostly beasts of burden like oxen or horses. Some cows were kept for milk and cheese and a small flock of sheep for their wool, sold for cash or bartered. Only very occasionally was animal meat eaten. The lack of sufficient feed for the animals over the winter was a constant problem. The prize beasts lived alongside the family usually under the same roof and were nursed through the winter on coarse grass and broom. Often the animals had literally to be carried to the fields the following spring, being so weak with hunger. The time in which the beasts were put out to pasture was known as the *'Lifting'*. Any surplus animals which could not be sold or bartered were as a last resort killed and salted for the winter. Poultry were kept for their eggs and fowl were kept as part of the rent. The old Scottish Parliament had produced various acts during the 17th century to encourage agricultural improvement. One such improvement was enclosing the land, but not only was it left up to the individual proprietors as to whether or not they should enclose, but the social upheaval it would cause to the wide spread runrig system of farming, ensured the act was doomed to failure.[73] Instead it was the great famine of 1699 and the political union with England in 1707 which proved to be the catalysts for improvement.

Very slowly new methods, equipment and techniques were introduced, but it was only after the failed Jacobite rebellion of 1745 that agricultural improvements moved into anything like top gear. Land was drained, hedges and walls enclosed the drained parks, and the patchwork effect with which we are so familiar slowly began to emerge. New crops, like wheat and potatoes, were widely grown. The new farm machinery and crop rotations promised to improve production and efficiency. By the end of the 18th century great improvements had been made and the speed of the changes were only going to increase, but there was still a long way to go.

There was a down side to the improvements. This involved the break up of the old fermtoun communities and the clearing from the land of the small farmers, cotters and crofters as their small holdings were consolidated into much larger farms. The old fermtoun communities were almost self sufficient; they would utilise everything they produced on the land. The wives and daughters would scour, card and spin the wool from their own sheep. They would then dye and weave it to produce their own cloth. The cloth would then be made into hodden grey or tartan clothing. Hides from their cattle would be tanned for leather and tallow would be converted for use as candles. The men would spend the long winter nights making brogues and horse furniture both for themselves and as for use as barter goods. Very little if anything was ever wasted and little was bought in from outside the fermtoun. Very little cash changed hands. People survived by bartering their labour or the labour of their families.

One of the most important places in the fermtoun would have been the dung heap. Prior to liming, both human and animal effluent were the only fertiliser available. The waste would be piled onto the dung heap which was usually just outside the front door and spread on the infield areas of the farm. Then as now some people resisted change. In the case of the fermtoun communities, they knew from bitter experience that famine and destitution were only a couple of failed crops away. It was all right for the likes of Campbell of Ardkinlass and Graham of Meiklewood to experiment with their crops, they could afford the losses. The people of the fermtouns and small farms knew their very existence was at stake.

Small farmers on the carse were still living in conditions which could best be described as medieval as late as 1785. The new improved farming methods required larger single occupancy farms, therefore the small farm holdings and fermtouns had to be broken up, with those who formerly had some small stake in the land becoming landless agricultural labourers, accommodated in the new villages like Gargunnock or moving their families to Stirling or further afield to Glasgow and the Clyde valley. It was very much a case of social engineering as the larger landowners simply made it impossible for people to remain on the land, at the same time, offering long leases or selling feus, in locations where they wished the people to settle.[74]

Although in many cases the people were unhappy at the changes, with many of them still entrenched in old traditional methods, the improvements were to prove a great success, with the material living standards of all the people rising considerably over the next couple of generations. Some ghosts of the old fermtouns can still be glimpsed in the place names which were retained by some of the new consolidated farms and can be seen on later maps. Places like Patrickston, Myreton and Spittleton were all former fermetoun communities. At the south western edge of the present day village there is a field still called the Lang Rig.

Conditions Improve

By the late 1770s, the new Gargunnock village was well established with the villagers becoming organised and settled into their community. It was a time of expansion and the people would have been hard at work improving the farms by building dykes, drainage ditches and clearing the old outfield areas as they were brought into cultivation. Wages were rising and the newly built houses in the village saw a vast improvement in the standard of housing.[75] There were also signs of the landless labourers becoming organised and challenging the power base of the landowners, particularly the small feuars. At this time Gargunnock held an annual Horse Race, the expenses being met by public subscription. In March 1776, the organisers found they had a sum left over after paying the bills. At a public meeting it was decided that the extra money would be spent on buying a drum and a horn and to appoint a drummer annually, there being only one clock in the village. The idea was that the drummer would waken the village at 5 a.m with the drum if it was dry, the horn if it was wet. A second call would happen at 9 p.m. In the springtime the drummer also called to warn the villagers to take in their chickens while people worked in their gardens. The drummer was paid by public subscription.[76]

A committee of eight men was formed to manage the affairs of the drummer and soon began to dabble in village politics; they called themselves the Council and their leader the Provost, much to the chagrin of the feuars. The landowners insisted that only a feuar could be Provost, but the tenants dug their heels in and eventually won the right to be a Provost. There is still a house at the top of the village brae known as Provost Park. The drum and horn is, with the permission of the trustee of the late Miss Viola H. Stirling CBE, currently in the safe keeping of the Smith Institute and Art Gallery in Stirling.

By the late 18th century a considerable portion of the Gargunnock parishioners lived in the village itself, but the majority continued to rely on agriculture for their living and were mostly employed as agricultural labourers working on the new enlarged farms. A number of tradesmen were operating from Gargunnock, attract-ed by the commissions available from the new larger farms and their labourers who now had to hire specialist skills. James McNair was a tailor, we know Mr Abercromby was a cooper, Robert McNair and George Patterson were shoemakers or souters as they were called, Andrew McIlhose and John and Archibald Stirling were all weavers, James Craig was a mason and John Brown a wright. There was at least one Inn keeper as well as the village stalwarts, the Minister, the Rev. William Martin, the School Master John Miller and the miller himself, but there were still no butchers or Fleshers as they were called and no grocer. These goods

The Gargunnock Drum and Horn

The Gargunnock Drum and Horn which awoke and sent to bed many generations of Gargunnock folk. The cartographers of the Ordnance Survey found them none too melodic. Both are now in the safe keeping of the Smith Art Gallery and Museum in Stirling.

were brought into the village by packmen carrying their wares on the backs of a trail of horses. There was intriguingly a Mr William Leckie who is listed as being a merchant, though what line of business he was in is not mentioned.[77]

It was probably about 1770/75 that James McNair arrived in Gargunnock Village itself, though, the McNair family appear to be natives of the Parish and there was a McNair family headstone in Gargunnock Kirkyard dating back to 1692.[78] As a tailor, James McNair would have been attracted into Gargunnock Village by its growing population and captive market for his services. Whereas in the old fermtouns the people were just about self sufficient, in the new villages they had to rely on tradesmen whom they paid with their cash wages for their services. Again, the minister in his Statistical Account alluded to the shifting parish population:

> 'It appears there has been little variation in the population of the parish for many years. The cotton mills at Balfron and Down, and the great demand at Glasgow a few years ago for weavers, masons and day labourers, considerably diminished the number of souls in this parish. The hope of regular employment and better wages, enticed several families to settle in those places, where young and old were constantly employed. By the late stagnation in trade, many have been compelled to return. Additions made to some farms and the spirit of improvement prevailing among the heritors, which has led them to keep a great part of their lands in their own possession, have banished a great many inhabitants from the dryfields, where the ruins of many cottages are to be met with; but in the mean time the village of Gargunnock, which in the memory of some still alive, "consisted of only 3 or 4 houses", now contains about 400 souls.'

Between 1755 and 1793 the Parish had in fact lost over 13% of its population. However, the village of Gargunnock itself had grown, as many of the banished inhabitants of the dismantled fermtouns and small farms settled in it.[79] After the battle of Culloden in 1746, it was decided to survey the whole of Scotland for military purposes. The resulting series of maps are known collectively as Roy's Map, named after a lowland Scot, General William Roy, who was the driving force behind the project. Gargunnock village, is shown on the map as two small strips of houses on either side of the military road. Each of the houses has a garden behind and the Kirk and Manse are of course shown. Unfortunately, the village is not only on the very edge of one map, it is also on the edge where four maps join, so it is difficult to get a clear picture of the whole parish. What the map does confirm is that by the 1750s, Gargunnock village had expanded at the expense of the old fermtoun communities.

By the time the Minister of Gargunnock was writing his account of the parish, the improvements had filtered through to most of the populace. The older parishioners were surprised by the increase in the standard of living and the circumstances of the young folk in comparison to their own younger days. The village of the 1790s consisted of about 400 souls occupying 90 houses, mostly single storey with thatched roofs. Each feu had a narrow, but quite long garden, in which the people grew small quantities of potatoes, kail, peas and beans. They may also have had the odd sheep or even a cow. The main source of fuel was coal, imported into the parish from Bannockburn 10 miles distant and peat was always available from the carse.

The recognition of the importance of good roads was another example of the mood

The Dryfields and Carse of Gargunnock Parish 1817

This section of the Stirlingshire map by Grassom shows the majority of the dryfields and carse of Gargunnock Parish. Surveyed about 1816 and printed in 1817, the map shows the turnpike road to Dumbarton bypassing the village Main Street.

of improvement which was still sweeping the country. We have already seen how the old medieval track that passed through the village was upgraded to a military road, some time around 1755. According to the Minister in his Statistical Account of 1793, a plan to upgrade it to a turnpike road had been announced. The Turnpike Trusts were formed specifically to improve the standard of the roads and were regarded as an investment. The new or improved roads had tollgates and charged users a fee for travelling on them. The road from Stirling to Dumbarton was built or improved between 1793 and 1796. When the road builders reached Gargunnock Village they looked at the gradient and decided to circumnavigate the hill feature on which the village stands. A new bridge was built to the north of the old bridge and a new stretch of road built between the new bridge and Leckie. The line of the road now came from Stirling and Touch, down the hill past the Manse and the Kirk, across the Square and James McNair's property, creating a small triangle of ground on the south, between the old and new Gargunnock bridges and carried on towards Leckie and Kippen, bypassing the village Main Street.[80]

It was thought locally that the building of Leckie Mansion in 1834 was the reason why the road was diverted to the north of the village, but this is obviously not the case. The Grassom map of Stirlingshire published in 1817 clearly shows the road bypassing the village, almost twenty years before the mansion was built. The reason for the road bypassing the village, was simply the steep gradient on which the village was built. An ever increasing number of horse-drawn vehicles was expected to be using the new road and the old route through the village would have been a hard pull on the way up and a dangerous descent on the way down. However, the building of Leckie Mansion in the 1830s was probably the reason the village Main Street was turned into a cul de sac. According to the minister, Rev James Robertson, the best inn on the road was in Gargunnock, it is described as being, *'kept in good order and remarkably clean and neat, a circumstance not very common in such establishments.'* Unfortunately, he didn't mentioned exactly where in the village the inn was located.

By the end of the 18th century much of the severity and strictness of the old Kirk was a thing of the past, but the Minister and his Elders still presented a formidable force in the lives of the parishioners. A glance through Gargunnock Kirk Session records makes fascinating reading as sinful parishioners are compeared to appear before the Session to be interrogated and rebuked for their actions. The records of the Kirk Sessions have been called the greatest untapped source of Scottish Social History. Numerous cases of adultery, drunkenness, swearing, Sabbath breaking and most of all, fornication continue to fill the pages as the Kirk Elders, sometimes requiring the judgment of Solomon, attempted to punish the wrongdoers and find fathers for impregnated lassies. An enormous amount of time and effort was spent in apportioning blame and making individuals accountable and responsible for their illegitimate children. In addition to the moral example, the Elders were trying desperately to alleviate the pressure on the rapidly becoming overstretched Kirk Poor Fund, which would be required to pick up the burden of the unmarried mother and her baby. Some things never change, the story sounds all too familiar today.

Women seldom got a mention in the old records unless they had brought themselves to the attention of their male betters, usually in the form of the Kirk Session. Unmarried pregnancy and slander were the two most usual methods for a woman to get herself noticed. Some such Gargunnock heroines were, Isabel Micklhose, called a vile slanderer. Christian Ure aged 23 in the village of

New Leckie Mansion House

Built by Dr Charles Graham Moir, the new mansion house is in the old English baronial style.Completed about 1834. Dr Moir had the old road from Gargunnock to Kippen blocked off at the western end of the village, thereby creating a cul-de-sac. The building is currently undergoing conversion into luxury flats.

Gargunnock, another slanderer. Isabella Miller, spouse to George Patterson, again a slanderer. Marjory Kerr, Rosie Graham and Janet Miller we came across earlier with their witchcraft trials. Some exceptions to the rule were the noble ladies of the parish, Agnes Smith and Marion Stewart receiving their pensions, Isabelle and Margaret Harvie, Kate Cram and Margaret Ure were some of the early feuars of Gargunnock Village.

The character of the Gargunnock parishioners of 1790s generally appear to be better than those of the sister and her relations in the earlier story. The Minister of Gargunnock praised his flock for seldom needing to be chastised and described their character, manners and customs as:

> 'The character of the inhabitants of this parish is sobriety. They profess to fear God, and honour the King. In deportment they are grave, and in their speech considerate. They are remarkably attached to the institutions of religion, and all of them, (22 persons excepted), worship together at the parish church. (About 800.) Young and old are distinguished for polite attention to strangers. Men of superior rank may have a respectful bow from everyone they meet; for people here have not been taught the new doctrine of liberty and equality. It is seldom there are social meetings. Marriages, baptisms and the conclusion of harvest, are the only time of feasting. At these times there is much unnecessary expense. Marriages usually happen in April and November. The month of May is cautiously avoided. A principal tenant's son or daughter has a crowd of attendants at marriage and the entertainment lasts for two days at the expense of the parties. The company at large pays for the music.'[81]

The Kirk continued to control the movement of people in and out of the parish through the issue of testificates or testimonials. Every newcomer into the parish was still required to produce such a testificate attesting to their good character, signed by their former minister. This was another attempt at minimising the possible claims on the parish poor funds, though by the late 1790s, the increasingly mobile population and the various splits within the church itself, were making this more and more difficult.

By 1796, the Napoleonic Wars were in full swing and some desperate food shortages meant top prices could be had for most crops. The costs of produce and labour were then as they are today, dictated largely by the laws of supply and demand. Farmers could afford to pay top wages for good workers and of course the farm workers took full advantage of the situation while it lasted. Labour shortages caused by demands for men from both the forces and industry operating at full capacity meant workers could pick and chose their masters. For farm workers the rates depended on whether you were a day worker or a permanent farm servant and if you were male or female. Sometimes the cost of food or victuals as it was called and accommodation was included. Generally, a living-in male farm servant could expect a wage of £7.10s to £10 per year. Female servants were paid £4 per year. Male day labourers who were considered less skilled than farm servants, would receive between 9d and 1s per day (5 new pence) plus victuals. At busy times of the farming year the daily rate increased to 1s 6d or 1s 8d.[82]

In Gargunnock Village the day workers were called to the fields by the sound of the pipes or the beating of a drum. Whereas 30 or 40 years previously cash would have been a very small fraction of the farm workers' pay, now the largest portion was paid in cash, with the farm workers, particularly the day labourers, paying for their food and other necessities like fuel, which would previously have been provided for them. In Gargunnock parish the price of the provisions would vary according to the demand at Stirling market, but on average in 1796, the following could be bought: oats at 15s (75p) per boll, peas and barley meal 10s per boll (140lbs), eggs at 4d (2p) per dozen, butter 12s (60p) per stone, best cheese 5s (25p) per stone.[83]

Like conditions generally, the diet of the ordinary people had improved considerably in the previous thirty or forty years, although oats were still very much the staple, eaten as a porridge or baked on a girdle over a fire into bannocks. Potatoes were grown and eaten in great quantities. They had been cultivated in the county for the best part of 50 years. Initially they were regarded with some suspicion and fed to the cattle. Yet the cultivation and acceptance of this crop was probably the single greatest agricultural improvement for the ordinary working man. The introduction of grasses for cattle feed meant many more beasts could be kept through the winter and as a result the price of meat fell. Much more meat was being eaten, whereas formerly meat would only be eaten on a special occasion, or on the accidental demise of a beast. Barley, peas, eggs, butter, cheese, poultry, and fish from the Forth, all added some variety. Kail, a form of cabbage, was the most common vegetable eaten, but other garden greens added some variety.

The improved communication in the form of the new roads meant all kinds of goods could be transported around the country much more easily. Until very recently the usual drink would have been ale made from barley, but tea, formally a delicacy for the gentry, was now used by all, sometimes laced with a little whisky to help counteract the bad effects of the tea. Wheat bread was also available for those who could afford it.[84]

Clothing was another yardstick by which the Gargunnock parishioners' conditions could be judged and at last the ordinary person had a few coppers left over to treat themselves to the odd ribbon or cotton shirt. The improvements saw the disappearance of the Guid Blue Bunnet to be replaced by the more genteel hat and homespun hodden-grey by suits of English broadcloth. The minister thought it remarkable that there was only one wig in the entire parish. Similarly the black bonnet and cloak, once the guidwife's pride and joy, was now also being worn by her servant lassies. This new finery would be kept for Sundays or a visit to the market in Stirling, for the remainder of the time men would wear homespun clothes made by their wives and daughters. The children and young unmarried women went unshod all week. The lassies would carry their shoes most of the way to Kirk then stop by the burn to wash their feet before putting on their good stockings and shoes and flounce into the Kirk, hoping to catch the eye of their beaux. By general agreement people of the times regarded themselves as better clothed and fed than their forefathers.[85] It must have been a cause for great satisfaction to know that the once ever present threat of deprivation and starvation, brought on by a failed harvest, had finally been lifted from their lives.

Agriculture was now regarded as a science and farmers were actively encouraged to experiment with new crops and crop rotations in an effort to maintain the improving standard in farming. General Henry Fletcher Campbell, Laird of Boquhan and one of the chief heritors of Gargunnock was one of the leading exponents of agricultural improvements. Over a prolonged period he invested considerable amounts of money in improving his own policies, at times amounts which far exceeded his rents. A long term policy of improvements was begun in 1780 with the dryfields of Boquhan barony being enclosed. Over 50 day labourers were employed in planting, hedging, draining and ditching. Considerable effort was put into removing any obstructions to the plough in the fields, roads were built between farms and the employment these works brought helped minimise the loss to the small cotters who lost their homes and land in the process.[86] In 1794, he started a farmers' club in the parish, perhaps the first in Scotland and in 1807 the General bequeathed it the sum of £500 sterling. Eleven local parishes were to benefit from the money.

In 1798, as part of a nation-wide survey of agriculture, a Mr Beeches produced a report on the state of agriculture in Stirlingshire. This detailed survey highlighted the improvements made already and the obstacles to further improvement. In the space of about 40 odd years, the industry had transformed itself from one of subsistence farming to one which regularly produced significant surpluses. Those farmers who adopted the improved farming methods, introduced the new crop rotation, improved drainage and bought the new machinery, found more acreage could be kept in cultivation longer, therefore producing more yield. The new machinery allowed more acreage to be managed with less manpower, therefore overheads were reduced and productivity went up. The improved land itself doubled and trebled in value as increased rents could be demanded by the owners. The land valuation of the parish doubled from £1500 to £3000 in the space of 30 years.[87]

Although much progress had been made, Beeches highlighted problem areas throughout the county which could be improved still further. The profusion of small farms, absentee landlords, attachment to traditional farming methods and lack of investment were cited as the main obstacles to continued improvement. On some of the small farms in the carse and hilly areas the farmers were still using the old Scots plough. He also commented on the standard of butter and cheese. He thought one could tell what fuel was used by the house in which the item was made. He thought that whereas peat and coal might make an excellent fire, they did nothing to enhance the taste of the butter or cheese.[88]

John Murdoch's House

In 1796, John Murdoch Jnr, son of John Murdoch, tenant farmer in nearby Beild of Leckie Farm, bought a portion of James McNair's feu for the princely sum of £8 sterling. The money was being put into what was the safest investment even then, property. Not only was it a good investment, but it was a step up the social ladder from tenant farmer to property owner. The portion John Murdoch bought was described as follows:

'All and whole that part of James McNair's feu in Gargunnock adjoining the new highway or turnpike road leading through Gargunnock and the road there from to Kippdarroch. Measuring twenty nine feet along the last mentioned road and turning from the north east corner westward forty four feet, then south to the new highway the whole forming a right angle to the front of the property, the south being slightly broader than the north due to the aforementioned roads not forming a perfect right angle. The whole property is bounded on the south by the new highway, to the east by the road to Kippdarroch and to the north and west by the remaining feu belonging to James McNair.'

This is exactly the plot of land on which today's Trelawney Cottage stands. Also included in the transaction was the triangular portion of ground across the new road to Leckie and which now contains the Memorial Fountain and Garden. The only additional burden put on the property by McNair was that John Murdoch was to allow him, if he so wished, to build a house adjacent to Murdoch's and to allow him to rest the roof of the building on the western gable of Murdoch's house.[89] This is confirmation that at the time of the feu transaction, Murdoch intended to build a house on the property. From subsequent documents relating to the property, it is clear that John Murdoch did indeed build the house. It is unclear however, exactly when he built the house. It is more than likely that the house was erected soon after the land was purchased. John Murdoch was obviously

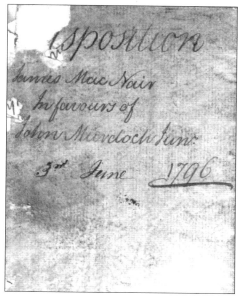

The McNair Disposition of 1796.

wealthy enough to buy the property, £8 sterling was roughly the equivalent of eight months salary for a male farm servant at the time. He would also have had to finance the construction of the house, which was even then no small expense. The present house conforms exactly to the style and construction methods of the late 18th early 19th century. A number of the other houses around the Square appear to have been built about the same time.

The exact reason for Murdoch building the house is unclear, though it was probably either for agricultural labourers who would be accommodated off the Beild farm or in anticipation of his marriage. Unfortunately, the marriage records in the parish registers are not complete for the period in which we would expect to see him being married. There is however, an entry in the birth register for John Murdoch and his spouse Jean Evan, a son named John, born on 21st September 1800. A clue as to the possible marriage date of John and Jean Murdoch can be found if we look at the birth dates of their children. There was once a system of naming children in Scotland which was once almost religiously adhered to. It is known today as the Scottish naming pattern and it went something like this. The first born son was named after the father's father. The second son was named after the mother's father. The third son was named after the father. The first daughter was named after the mother's mother. The second daughter after the father's mother. The third daughter named after the mother. Subsequent children were named after the parent's sisters and brothers. If you imagine all the children following the same pattern, each family could have four or five children all named after the same person. The same names appear in the same families for generation after generation.

If we apply the naming pattern to John Murdoch Jnr, then his son, John, should be his first born. He would therefore probably have been married sometime between 1797 and 1799, which would fit with the suggestion that the house was built for his bride. Unfortunately, it would appear that John's father died around the same time and if he had intended to move in to the new house, this apparently changed John's plans. The opportunity to succeed his father and take on an established working farm, would be too good to pass up. In the Gargunnock parish register of births for a number of his subsequent children, John is listed as the tenant of Beild of Leckie Farm.[90] This may have been the start of the property in Gargunnock village being let to tenants, with the house being seen simply as an investment.

The Nineteenth Century

From about 1812 the entire country went into a serious economic depression. Demand for goods related to the war years fell and in the mills and factories many people were laid off work. The unemployment situation was made worse by the increasing population, immigration and the return of the victorious British regiments from the Napoleonic wars. Many of which were immediately disbanded, throwing tens of thousands of soldiers into an already saturated employment market. The economic situation affected the wages of those who remained in work, many having to accept reductions of 25% to 50%. Adding to the people's problems were the Corn Laws, a government measure aimed at keeping the price of grain artificially high in order to placate their voters who were landowners and farmers. This of course meant that the end product, bread or bannocks' also remained high at a time when wages were falling. Farmers had watched crop prices plummet from their former highs. Oatmeal lost almost a third of its price between 1812 and 1819, and would have fallen further without government intervention. Since political power lay in the hands of the landowners the hated Corn Laws remained on the statute book for years. In 1817, despite the Corn Laws and perhaps as a consequence of the depression, John Murdoch gave up farming at Beild of Leckie and moved into the village and presumably his house on the Square. He disposed of the property in May 1819, but the value of his £8 investment had multiplied by over 20 times. James sold the land and dwelling house to Mr John McCulloch, a toll contractor at Campsie Muir, for £166 Sterling. It is in this disposition document that the dwelling house is first mentioned. Unfortunately no specific date is included. When referring to the dwelling house it simply states 'that dwelling house built by John Murdoch some time ago'.[91]

A Toll Contractor was the person who had successfully bid for the lease of a stretch of toll road. The position was offered at a public auction every year and the successful bidder kept the income from the tolls. There was supposed to be a distance of 6 miles between toll bars, but they were often much shorter. The new road from Stirling to Dumbarton, through the carse, was originally a toll road. Much to the delight of the hauliers and carriers, tolls were eventually abolished in 1878.[92] The next time the property is documented is in 1823. John McCulloch gave joint ownership of the property to his wife Ann MacDonald, but only for the duration of her lifetime. This was known as liferent and was simply a legal device to allow a spouse or children some security of tenure, enabling them to occupy a property after the owner had died and the property had passed to his heir.[93] The house would normally be left to the eldest son and the land or property would be burdened by the liferent. Although she was effectively joint owner, the liferenter could not dispose of the property or any part of it.

Although we know when John McCulloch Snr died,[94] unfortunately, we do not know if he or his wife, ever occupied the house. It is most likely that the house was bought as an investment and let to tenants. Under normal circumstances the toll contractor lived in the Toll House, unless he employed someone to collect the tolls on his behalf. The family are not listed as being anywhere in the village in the 1841 census, and because we cannot positively identify the house, there is no way of identifying who was occupying the it at the time. There are a couple possibilities, including a family called Hardie, but no way of telling for certain.

By the winter of 1827, the original feuar James McNair and his wife Jean Morrison were well into their old age and living in reduced circumstances. James and his wife were recognised by the Kirk Session as a couple who might need some help from the Poor Fund. The Session awarded the family a cart load of coal, but before it could be delivered, they discovered that one of James's sons had already given his parents a load of coal. The Session therefore decided to delay the award, judging that the McNair's need was no longer as pressing.[95] Before it could decide what to do with the load of coal, James McNair died on 11th March, 1827, aged 76. The Session decided to award the family the price of the load of coal in cash to assist with funeral expenses. James's funeral would have been a major event in the parish. It was once asserted that in Scotland, the family burial plot with headstone, hearth in the home and seat in the kirk, were the three fundamentals which helped cement families together. The Kirk had been trying for centuries to break the old customs surrounding funerals, 200 years after the General Assembly proclamation about the conduct of wakes, the Gargunnock Minister had to admit that:

> 'The manner of conducting funerals needs much amending. From the death to the internment, the house is thronged by day and night, and the conversation is often unsuitable to the occasion. The whole parish is invited at 10 o'clock in the forenoon of the day of the funeral, but it is soon enough to attend at 3 o'clock afternoon. Everyone is entertained with a variety of meat and drink. Not a few return for the dirge, and sometimes forget what they are doing, and where they are. Attempts have been made recently to provide a remedy for this evil; but old customs are not easily abolished.'[96]

James McNair was buried beside his ancestors in Gargunnock Kirkyard. Sometime later his son John McNair, replaced the old family headstone originally erected in 1692. Curiously, on the new tombstone James McNair's death is given as 1825. On James's death, heritable possession of the feu went to his second born son James McNair Jnr, he had already transferred the property to him in 1822.[97] This was not unusual considering the advanced age of James McNair Snr. The property was burdened with the life rents of both himself and his wife Jean Morrison. Heritable property was generally settled on the sons and only as a last resort were daughters made heritors. If there was more than one daughter the property was usually divided and they became heir portioners. James McNair did have an older son, William McNair, but it would appear that he had been left out of his father's will.

The period between 1800 and 1840 is really something of a dark age as far as the occupants of the Murdoch house is concerned. There are few sources available which would allow us to identify exactly who was living in the property, though it continued to be owned by John Murdoch and later by John McCulloch. As far as the Parish and Village are concerned, a slow but steady growth in population took place in these years. By the early 1840s, the population was a little over 900, an increase of just under 10% since 1793 when it stood at 830.[98] The increase was almost entirely centred on the Village itself, as the smaller farms continued to be consolidated and various tradesmen moved into the Village to service the community. The population of the village now stood at 466 and outnumbered that of the country or rural population, which stood at 422. In 1826, Glenfoyle distillery opened at Dasherhead and would provide employment for the village over the next 100 years or so.[99] A new toll road through the carse had been built and although quicker, it lost much in the way of scenery in comparison to the old Dumbarton road which passed through the village.

Nationally, two major events which affected the population of both the Parish and Village took place at the beginning of the 1830s. In the summer of 1832, the dreaded cholera struck the inhabitants of nearby Stirling. The new plague, which seemed to be of almost biblical proportions, first arrived in the country from Asia, the previous autumn. The earliest known case was reported in the north of England in October 1831. The disease appeared to leap large parts of the country leaving some places totally unaffected. It would suddenly appear in a town or village and the deaths would begin almost immediately. The symptoms were vomiting and diarrhoea, giddiness and cramps. The victim's face became shrunken, the eyes sunken and wild. The whole body turned blue, purple and black, death occurred within hours of the first signs of the symptoms. The suddenness of the onset of the disease and the percentage of fatalities (usually about 70%) appalled and terrified everyone, no matter

A young girl dies of cholera.

their social standing. It was not just the horrible symptoms and near certainty of death which horrified people, but the fact that no one knew how it was contracted or how the disease was transmitted, therefore, no one knew how to prevent it. Its seemingly sporadic and random attacks added to the uncertainty and people could only watch and wait as it sometimes crept and at other times leapt across the country. In January 1832, Stirling set up a Board of Health in response to the emergency and dispatched two local doctors to Edinburgh to find out what if any precautions could be taken.[100]

It appeared to the Stirling doctors that the illness prevailed in the dirtiest most overcrowded parts of the town and their recommendations and precautions were based around this premise. Immediately on their return, the doctors set out their findings and recommendations. They advised that any wandering vagrants or tramps be expelled from towns and villages. Business between towns and villages was to be kept at an absolute minimum. Clothing parcels were collected and soup kitchens set up for the poor as they were considered the most likely source of the disease. The idea was that it would be better to help the poorest people who were most at risk to resist the disease, thereby reducing the risk of infection for the more affluent sections of the community. All buildings were to be washed down both inside and out. Cholera hospitals were set up and District committees established to oversee the precautions and report to the Board of Health.[101]

Gargunnock likewise acted on the recommendations of the Stirling doctors. Additionally, the villagers posted sentries on all the roads and tracks leading into the village to prevent people they regarded as a risk from entering. A cholera hospital was set up and several sick nurses engaged. A soup kitchen was established for the poor of the village. Between 36 and 38 persons were daily supplied with a penny loaf and a chopin of soup mixed with butcher meat. Children received half the quantity. The single most effective precaution taken by the villagers of Gargunnock, although they never realised it at the time, was covering the open sewer which ran the length of the main street.[102] By the end of February, as far as the people were concerned, everything had been done that could be done. They could now only wait and watch as the plague closed in on the parish. The progress of the plague, including the terrifying statistics recording the fatalities, appeared in the local newspapers. Life had to continue of course, with fields to sow, but always with an eye open for strangers or neighbours suddenly becoming sick.

On 3rd February a confirmed case of cholera had been diagnosed at Kirkintilloch, only 14 miles away. Further reports firstly from Dollar, then Alloa, confirmed fatalities from the plague. Finally, at the beginning of June, there was a confirmed case of cholera in Stirling. Mr Charles McFarlane, a dealer in old clothes, who resided in St John Street, was the first victim. His illness began at mid-day and he died the following day. An Irish girl was next, then a cobbler named MacDonald. As reported in the Stirling Advertiser, all three victims were in perfect health only hours before the onset of the first symptoms. Between June and August, 60 citizens of Stirling town died from the disease.[103] The closest case to Gargunnock was a resident of Blair Drummond, who died after visiting his sick mother in Stirling. Happily, there were to be no cases in Gargunnock. The appalling disease was carried by water and food contaminated by effluent, so the covering of the communal open sewer and the virtual quarantine imposed on the village undoubtedly helped spare the villagers the prospect of a ghastly death. It was a terrifying period for not only the folk of Gargunnock, but for the entire nation. It is estimated that the 1831/2 outbreak of cholera cost in excess of 10,000 Scottish lives.[104]

James McNair inherited the feu on his father's death and in February 1830, began the construction of a new single storey building on his property. He took advantage of the burden mentioned in the original disposition of 1796 and rested the roof on the western gable of the two storey house built by Murdoch. The new single storey building was in fact two separate houses. The erection of a second storey sometime later, converted what was Mr McCulloch's detached house into the terrace of three houses we see today. In May 1830, James McNair married a Kippen girl called Janet Stirling and by May 1832, Janet was heavily pregnant with their first child. Unfortunately, Janet died in childbirth, the baby was delivered alive, but died a few months later. 105 James himself died only a couple of years later in 1834. On his death the feu passed to his younger brother John McNair, a mason, living in the village.[106]

The second event of national importance was the debate on the reform of voting rights. Between the end of the Napoleonic conflict and 1830 an ever increasing ground-swell of public opinion favoured a reform of the political voting system. The question of reform had first been raised by the events of the French Revolution 40 years earlier, but the Napoleonic war had put the subject on the back burner. Over the same period the mainly Tory governments had resisted any political change. By 1830, the pressure for change was such that even town councils like Stirling were involved in the debate. In 1828, the Town Council was split 10 to 10 on the subject, with the Provost casting his vote with the reformers to end the deadlock.[107] There were great celebrations all over the district at the defeat of the anti-reformers. The vast majority of the people had no franchise, the right to vote being dependent upon a person's wealth.

In 1830, the Tories led by the Duke of Wellington (of Waterloo fame), lost a general election and a Whig (Liberal) government was elected. Led by Earl Gray, the Whigs embarked on the road which led, after many tribulations, to the Reform Act (Scotland) being passed in 1832. Although the Reform Act still left the vast majority of the population unfranchised, it was a small but significant step in the process towards universal suffrage. There was a surprising amount of political awareness within the communities considering how few people were eligible to vote. Between 1830 and 1832 many large reform meetings took place throughout the county, with many hundreds turning out to hear the speeches and lend their support. At these meetings Gargunnock had some representatives from the village Reform Association. On many such occasions there were processions with various bands and with banners held aloft by the many groups associated with the cause. In the middle of August 1832, Stirling held its Reform Jubilee to celebrate the passing of the bill.

A full account of the day can be found in the Stirling Journal of 16 August 1832. The Journal mentions the fact that all the villages, including Gargunnock, celebrated the event by erecting triumphal arches and decking them and the houses with flowers. On the morning of the Jubilee a procession left Gargunnock in a cloud burst and marched 5 miles to Stirling's King's Park, to be part of the larger celebrations being organised by Stirling. By the time they arrived at the park the sun had come out and the march through Stirling commenced, by way of King St, Baker St, the Bow, up the south side of Broad St, Church St and down the north side of Broad St, St Mary's Wynd and Bridge St, along Cowan St, Friars St and back to the park. The procession included the Provost and Town Council, Magistrates, Town Guild, Trade and Labour Associations, various Reform Associations and numerous marching bands playing martial music and patriotic airs. The procession was cheered by the vast majority of the population and was marred only by the occasional shower of rain.[108]

At the end of the parade the assembled masses remained in King's Park for the subsequent speeches. The fervour and numbers involved in the Reform campaign seem all the more remarkable when we consider it in the context of today's political lethargy. The overall effect of the bill itself on the number of people who could vote was minimal. The franchise was now given to men who owned or rented property over £10. When you consider that almost twenty years later you could rent a large house for £6,10s p.a. it puts the changes into context. Overall the number of voters on the Stirling roll was increased to 362, from a population of 9000.[109] When you realise that the people conducted their meetings with the threat of the recent cholera outbreak still hanging over them, the turnout and political fervour was nothing short of remarkable.

The house in Gargunnock which would become the Guest House has had a long association with drink and the sale of liquor, most definitely as early as 1851, but quite possibly before that. The property was let to various tenants during the 1820s and 30s and although we cannot establish it for certain, one intriguing possibility is that it was let to a Mr Robert Dykes. If that were the case, we could report a murder having taken place in the house. According to the *Stirling Journal* of the 25th November, on Saturday 20th November 1830,

'*Robert Dykes, a labourer, who also kept a public house in Gargunnock, died in consequence of the mortification of a wound on his head, which he had received eight days earlier in his house while drinking with a carter named Peter Ferguson. It is said that the parties quarrelled, owing to the deceased having taunted Ferguson with stealing on a former occasion, a pair of stockings from a line which was hanging across the apartment wherein they were then sitting. Ferguson who is generally considered a peaceable lad, is said to have immediately fired at the accusation cast upon him, and in the impulse of the moment, to have seized a stick which was accidentally lying near the fireplace, and to have struck the deceased a severe blow to the head, which subsequently confined him to the house. Dykes had for some time been working at Leckie House, and was known to Mr Moir, who missed him from his work, and on learning what had taken place, caused his head to be examined by a medical gentleman in the neighbourhood. From the alarming appearance of the wound, information of the scuffle was sent to the Sheriff Substitute of Stirlingshire, who along with the Fiscal, and a medical gentleman went by Gargunnock on Friday, and took a precognition into the circumstances of the case. In the meantime Dykes gradually became worse till he expired. On Saturday evening the body was examined in the presence of several medical gentlemen, who reported that the deceased died as a consequence of the wound having mortified. Ferguson has of course been apprehended, and lodged in Stirling jail, but rumour asserts that owing to the want of sufficient evidence, there will probably be great difficulty in proving the assault.*'

In the early 1840s, another Statistical Account was completed by the Parish Ministers. This account was known as the New or Second Statistical Account and followed very closely the guide lines of the first. Like its predecessor, it is both a snapshot of parish life at the time the account was written and a reflection of times recently past. In the case of this second account the time between Statistical Accounts is recorded. The Minister at the time was The Reverend, Mr James Laurie, born in 1778. He had been the Minister of Gargunnock since 1830.[110] This second account, although not as detailed as the first, is nonetheless a valuable insight into the changing lifestyles of the parishioners over the period. In his account the Mr Laurie records the changes in the Parish since the time of the first Statistical Account. His narra-tive records the ongoing improvements in most areas, with the standard of living of most parishioners continuing to improve. The most signifi-cant physical improvements were the new Toll Road from Stirling to Dumbarton. This new road followed the flat route through the carse and bypassed the village a half mile to the north. Although faster, the minister felt the

A coach and four is let through a Tollgate.

most scenic route was still the old road. The new single span suspension bridge across the Forth built by Colonel Graham of Meiklewood opened up a new route across the carse. The new wedge and stone drainage system improved the land already in cultivation and offered the opportunity to utilise more land in the future. Through this and other agricultural improvements the land in the parish had doubled in value since the last statistical account. Finally, the new mansion

Gargunnock Estate 1851

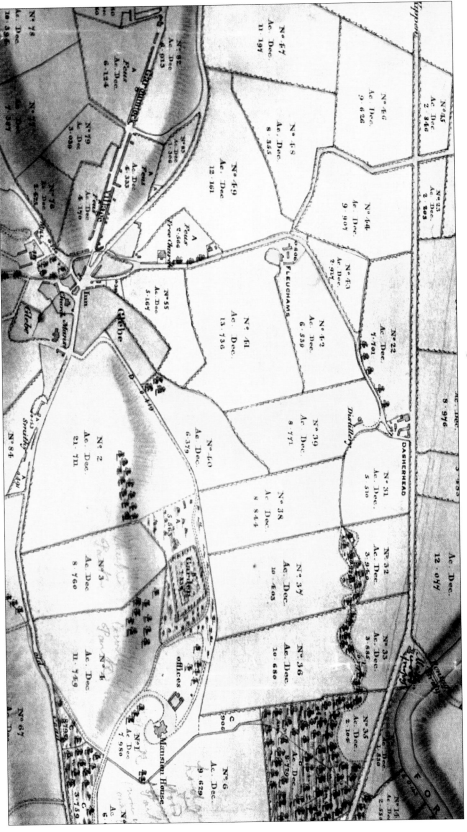

This plan of the Gargunnock Estate was commissioned by John S Stirling in 1851. It shows the estate completely enclosed after 100 years of improvements. Points of interest are the Meiklewood Pontage or Toll Bridge over the Forth. The old school house at the western edge of the village and the recently built Free Church at Foot O' Green.

houses of both the Moirs at Leckie and the Grahams at Meiklewood, lately built, are highlighted as examples of more enlightened and genteel times.

In 1841, there were three schools in the Parish, the parochial school founded in 1652, with its schoolmaster appointed by the session and whose salary in 1841 was £25. 13s 3½d per annum. Two un-endowed schools, one near the village which was well attended, the other some 2 miles away at Burnton which sat mostly in the winter. There was also an infant school which was run from the Manse by a Mrs Lawrie. In 1830, a parish library was established and another was available for the Sabbath school.[111] Although not regarded as improvements, the Minister also mentions that there were four alehouses and one distillery in the parish. The Minister wasn't to realise in his account that the parish population had passed its peak of 1,006 in 1831 and had begun to decline, a fall which would continue for the next 70 years.[112]

By the middle of the 19th century the Parish Poor Fund, once the mainstay of the poor, was in serious trouble. The strain began to show during the depression following the end of the Napoleonic wars with the influxes of immigrants from both the Highlands and Ireland overloading a system which depended on voluntary contributions at the Kirk door, mortcloth money and investments. Now it was the textile industry which employed tens of thousands in the towns and cities and tens of thousands more in the village cottages which was in depression. The final nail in the coffin came when the Church of Scotland split over patronage in 1843. The Disruption as it was known saw two out of every five ministers including the Moderator of the General Assembly, leave the established church and form the Free Church of Scotland. The congregations were also split on the matter and the new ministers of the Free Church took many of their old parishioners with them. If the Gargunnock school rolls are anything to go by, the parish was split almost in half.

Gargunnock had a new Free Church built at Foot O' Green with the Manse at the western extremity of the village and Free Church school on the south side of the square.[113] The loss of congregations to the established church meant a loss of contributions collected on a Sunday and although there had been other fractures of the established church, this disruption soon saw the end of the Church's official responsibility for the poor. In 1845 Parochial Boards took over the Poor Relief and although in many cases the faces on the new boards belonged to the same people who were members of the Kirk Session or the parish heritors, the old authority of the national established church was irretrievably broken.

The House 1849/1865

The house on the Square continued to be let to tenants. When its owner John McCulloch died on 7th April 1849 the house passed to his son, another John McCulloch, who was the contractor on the Toll Bar at Camlachie, near Glasgow.[114] During the 1851 census, the house was occupied by a Jane Hardie aged 46, who was listed as 'Keeping the House', obviously on behalf of John McCulloch. Also in the house was her son William Hardie, an 11 year old scholar and Alexander McNair, in residence, aged 4. The exact relationship between Jane Hardie and Alexander McNair is as yet unclear. However, as Alexander's mother Margaret Doig died when he was 6 months old, chances are he was simply being looked after by a neighbour.[115] The Hardie family had probably occupied the property since the previous Census of 1841. Although, as was stated earlier, we cannot pinpoint the house precisely, the family were certainly living in the immediate vicinity. Jane Hardie was the wife of Morris Hardie, a mason born in Gargunnock. Her maiden name was Lauder and she was born in St Cuthbert's parish, Edinburgh, about 1805. The couple were married in November 1830, in the Kirk at Gargunnock, both were aged 25.[116] By the time of the 1841 Census, the family has grown with the addition of four sons, all between nine and two years of age. Ten years later her husband was dead and most of her family had left the home.

The Census of 1851 is the first time we can accurately pinpoint the house. A combination of the census return and the subsequent disposal of the property by John McCulloch, identify the property as that which Jean Hardie is shown to be occupying in the 1851 census return. Four years later in the first Valuation Roll of 1855, the proprietor is listed as John McCulloch, Toll Keeper at Camlachie, but the property is let to and occupied by a Mr William Hardie, spirit dealer, for the princely sum of £6.5s per year. On the Stirling Valuation Roll, the property is described as a house and stable.[117] There appears to be no connection between William Hardie, spirit dealer, and Jane Hardie the former occupier. For the next few years the Valuation Rolls continue to list William Hardie as the tenant and occupier of the property.

A Lance Corporal of the 93rd 1852.

Like very many of his contemporaries, William Hardie joined the army. He served in the 93rd Highlanders, enlisting on 26th of October 1820.[118] In records held by the Museum of the Argyll and Sutherland Highlanders, at Stirling Castle, William is described as being 5ft 9 in tall. He had a dark complexion with a long face, brown hair and grey eyes. On his service records he is annotated as being a shoemaker to trade. The 93rd Highlanders were raised in 1799 with over one third of the recruits coming from the estate of the Duchess of Sutherland. Between 1780 and 1820, the regiment served in Guernsey, South Africa and America. During the war against the United States, a battle was fought at New Orleans on 8th January 1815. The regiment lost 116 killed, 359 wounded and 81 missing. The disastrous battle need never have been fought, a peace treaty having been signed at Ghent a few weeks before. Soon after New Orleans, the Regiment returned to the United Kingdom and was posted to Ireland. His first two years in the Regiment took William to various locations throughout Ireland including Cork, Armagh and Dublin.

The Regiment was then posted to the West Indies, arriving there over the period 14th December 1823 to 9th January 1824 and were to remain there until the spring of 1834. The colonies were broken down into four commands, Jamaica, Bahamas, Honduras and the Windward and Leeward Islands. The 93rd were attached to the latter which included posts at Trinidad, Tobago, Grenada, Barbados, St Lucia and Pigeon Is, St Vincent, Antigua and Monserrat. On arrival the 93rd were split into various detachments and taken by canoe or ship to their new duty stations. The Regiment would not be together again for over 10 years.

While posted around the islands the Highlanders would have coped with temperatures unlike anything they would have known previously. Likewise the 60 or 70 inches of annual rainfall and seasonal hurricanes would have been new experiences. The profusion of small commands would have added to the opportunity for promotion and in 1827, William was promoted from Corporal to Sergeant, but eight months later reduced in rank. Unfortunately the records do not state to what rank or for what reason. It was probably back to Corporal, his promotion being only a temporary or acting rank.[119]

The regiment found great difficulty in recruiting during their time in the West Indies. The posting was regarded by most soldiers as almost a death sentence. Almost all of the soldiers fell victim to the many tropical diseases prevalent in the tropics, many succumbed to them and were never to return home to Scotland.

Some locations were un-heathier than others. Pigeon Island was the worse having claimed 14 victims in two years, this from a detachment of no more than 20 soldiers at any one time. Although the figures are unreliable it would appear that the Regiment lost over 230 men while stationed in the West Indies, this from a total strength of about 670 men who served with the Regiment during the 10-year West Indian posting. The cause for most of the deaths could probably be attributed to the lack of sanitation and the failure to grasp the importance of clean water.

William Hardie managed to survive the unhealthy conditions, the boredom and the dangers of the sea voyage home. The 93rd Highlanders arrived back in the United Kingdom in early 1834 and were posted to Canterbury. Two years in England, followed by two years in Ireland, was all the Regiment was to have at home before being dispatched to Canada. In 1839, the French Canadians were in revolt and a number of Regiments including the 93rd were dispatched to put down the insurrection. The Regiment remained in Canada until 1848 when it finally returned to Scotland after an absence of 43 years.

On arrival back in Stirling, William Hardie took the opportunity to leave the regiment after 28 years service. On 28th November 1848, Hardie who gave his age as 44, married Jean McArthur, also aged 44, a vintner from Kippen.[120] The couple settled in Gargunnock and three years later during the 1851 Census, the couple are shown as living in village. William had reverted back to his old occupation and is working as a shoemaker.[121] Sometime between the Census of 1851 and 1855 William and Jean moved into the house belonging to John McCulloch and began selling spirits.

John McCulloch Jnr continued to own the property until 1857, when it was put to public roup. The sale was held in the Golden Lion Hotel in Stirling, on 16th October and the successful bid of £75 was made by Mr Charles Forsyth, former master shoemaker, then Postmaster in Gargunnock.[122] Charles and his wife Margaret, who was eleven years his junior, were both born in Gargunnock. On the 1851 Census return for the village, Charles is listed as a 50 year old master shoemaker, employing two men. Also living in the house with him was his wife, aged 39, and two house servants.[123]

Charles Forsyth appears to have been something of an entrepreneur and owned

A water-colour of Gargunnock Village about 1855. Although very picturesque the village was in fact in severe decline with many villagers leaving for the towns of the Clyde valley, North America, Australia and New Zealand. Probably at the suggestion of Charles Stirling of Gargunnock, spale basket makers from the north of England and Kirkcudbrightshire were invited to move into the area in an attempt to reverse the decline. The original painting is in the possession of the Gargunnock Kirk Session.

a number of properties throughout the village. He was also one of its first postmasters. The lane or loan towards the top of the village which leads from the main street to Leckie road is still called Charlie's Loan and was according to the Gargunnock Estate Chartulary, named after Charles Forsyth who owned Belton Cottage which faces onto the lane. Belton Cottage or an adjacent house was the location of the village post office while Charlie was the postmaster.[124]

The Stirling Observer *September 1857 advertising the house for sale.*

When Forsyth bought the property from McCulloch it was being run as a drinking establishment by William Hardie and his wife. So it appears to have been bought simply as another of Charles's investments. William Hardie is listed in the 1860 edition of *Slaters Trade Directory*, as one of four vintners in the village.[125] On the Ordnance Survey map of 1860, the building is annotated as being a Public House. The National Census of 1861, shows Jean Hardie in residence in the property and she is listed as being the wife of a spirit dealer. There is no sign of William Hardie on the return, being elsewhere on the night of the census. There are two carters living in the house as guests or boarders.[126] The Valuation Roll of 1865, lists the property as a Public House, owned by Mr Charles Forsyth and let to Mr William Hardie, spirit dealer, for £17.15s annually.[127]

The Years of Decline

The 30 years between 1840 and 1870 were in many ways a time of contradiction for the Parish and the Village. It saw the coming of the railways with the opening of Gargunnock Station on the Forth and Clyde railway route from Stirling to Balloch in 1856. The station itself was situated close to Dasherhead Farm and was the first and last stop from Stirling. Although there was initially an industrial/business aim for the line it never fulfilled its potential and was little more than a convenience for those who wished to go to the town. By 1857 the Royal Mail had arrived in the village and Gargunnock had its own Post Office situated initially in or near Belton Cottage. The post arrived at 12 noon and departed at 4 p.m.[128]

A new Public School opened on the Leckie road in 1858. The modern purpose built buildings with a house for the Schoolmaster were erected on a plot freely given by the then Laird of Gargunnock, Charles Stirling.[129] The buildings were to remain in service as a school until 1977 when a new village school opened near the old Free Church. Today the old school complex, which includes an extension built in 1911, is the village community centre.

In about 1857 the cartographers of the Ordnance Survey arrived in the village. In addition to mapping the area, they checked with the local dignitaries, such as the Lairds and the Minister as to the correct spelling and origins if known, of the local place names which would be shown on the map. The Minister at the time was the Reverend John Stark. Born in London, he was educated at the University of

Railway Station, Gargunnock.

Gargunnock Railway Station was opened in 1856 by the Forth and Clyde Railway Co. The station was adjacent to the site of the suspension bridge built by Graham of Meiklewood in 1832 and mentioned in the New Statistical Account. The Stationmaster's house, three chimneys of which can be seen through the trees, stands on the site of the suspension bridge toll gate house. Nearby, is the old smithy of Alexander Brown.

Glasgow and arrived in Gargunnock in 1844. A year later he married Isabella Crystal the daughter of Andrew Crystal the distiller at Dasherhead. John Stark was to be one of the longest serving Ministers in the history of the parish.[130] The Crystals were one of the oldest families in the parish, their name appearing in some of the very earliest parish records. In addition to taking the details of the local place names, the cartographers often included interesting facts or local customs associated with the place names. An interesting pen picture of Gargunnock village was included in their name books.

"The village is poor, most of the inhabitants being labourers and no trade of any kind is done in the neighbourhood. It consists mainly of one and two storey houses party thatched and partly slated. Generally they are in bad repair and many are ruinous".

The writer goes on to describe the custom of the Drum and Horn and sarcastically adds that the horn is not in the least musical to a stranger. He also noted that the old drummer was paid £2 p.a. raised by subscription. He closes by adding that the village has three public houses, two churches with their schools and manses, a post office and a corn and flour mill worked by water.[131]

However, despite the apparent advances mentioned by the minister, the Village and Parish were still in decline as natives continued to move away. The continuing exodus from the Parish can be put down to a number of factors. Handloom weaving and other cottage industries were in decline. The continuing mechanisation of agriculture meant less and less manpower was required. Higher wages in the towns and cities were attractive as were offers of cheap passages to the emerging colonies and the Americas. Offers of free land in plots unheard of in Scotland, must have been a tremendous lure for a generation brought up on stories of lands once held by their parents and grandparents. The descendants of Robert McNair were typical. Between 1851 and 1855 three out of four grandsons took advantage of assisted passage schemes and left the Parish, emigrating to Australia and New Zealand in search of a better life.[132] The standard of living in the Village continued to decline and a few years later the Lady of Gargunnock, Mrs Stirling, felt it necessary to organise a savings club in which the villagers saved for blankets and clothes.[133] The decline in the population would continue until well into the 20th century when it finally stabilised. Between 1831 when the population of the Parish peaked and 1911 when the figure finally stabilised at 543, the loss of population was just over 46%.[134]

The 1871 Census returns show the first appearance of families of Spale Basket Makers. This was a deliberate attempt to bring some cottage industry to a Village which appeared to be dying. By the early 1860s, the loss of population must have been readily apparent to anyone with an interest in the village. Certainly, the Laird of Gargunnock, would have seen a steady drop in his rents with a large portion of the village properties lying empty and decaying.

The spale basket makers came mostly from the north of England and Kirkcudbrightshire and were attracted to Gargunnock by the plentiful supply of young coppice oak, ash and hazel which was used in the making of their baskets. The baskets, which were mostly oval in shape and between 22 and 36 inches long, were sold mainly for carrying coal or potatoes, though a large customer was the firm of Coats of Paisley, the thread manufacturer.[135] Twenty years later the largest basket works and shop in the village belonged to a Mr Travis who arrived in

Main Street, Gargunnock.

The photograph was taken from the old bridge looking west. The children in the foreground are standing directly opposite what would become the current village shop. The man in the middle distance with the bicycle is standing outside what would become the Post Office.

Gargunnock with his brother. The shop and factory once stood in what is now the garden of the White House and employed 15 men. Another smaller establishment operated from a house on the north west side of the old Gargunnock Bridge. The basket makers worked a long day starting at 7 am and finishing at 9 pm. Over the next 40 odd years the industry would thrive in the village with a dozen or so families depending on it for their livelihood.[136] The arrival of the basket makers and the employment provided by the railway, the distillery at Dasherhead and McLaren's sawmill were probably the saving of the village.

The McLarens' are an old Gargunnock family who have lived in the village for around 200 years. One of the first was Archibald McLaren, a wright, who married Margaret Junkin about 1815. As was usual in those days the couple had a large family, ten children, four daughters and six sons. The sons all appear to have been involved in the family saw-milling business which by the mid 19th century, was one of the few opportunities for employment in the parish. At the height of their prosperity the McLarens' employed at least a half dozen local men on a permanent basis and probably as many again on seasonal contracts. The McLarens' were also local property developers owning numerous properties throughout the village. Descendants of Archibald McLaren still live in the village to this day.[137]

In 1866 Charles Forsyth decided to sell the house. As far as we can tell William Hardie was still occupying the property or he had been the previous year. He may have been hoping to remain in the house which is what happened the last time the house was sold. This time however the new owner, John Brown, was in the same line of business as Hardie. John Brown was born in St Ninian's parish about 1811 and at the time of the sale was already living and working in the village, being described as a vintner. He was a 45 year old married man, his wife Mary was six years older and had been born in Kincardine, Perthshire. Although John Brown was born in St Ninians, he moved to Kincardine prior to 1835. It was there that he met and married Mary Livingstone, with all the children born to the couple being born in Kincardine Parish.[138]

In the 1865 Valuation Roll, John Brown, Publican, is listed as living nearby, perhaps in the White House. He was renting the property for £9 p.a., from John Forrester, a farmer at Nether Carse. 139 John Brown bought the property from Charles Forsyth for £110. Confirmation that the property continued to be used as a Public House is in the 1871 Census, when John Brown is annotated as the Publican and Mary as a Publican's wife. The couple are living in the property with Robert Brown, their grandson aged 5.[140] The newly acquired property became known as Brown's Inn and later as Brown's Pub.[141]

John Brown's oldest son, Robert, was born in 1835. As a 45 year old widower he married 18 year old Catherine Dick, a domestic servant from Ballochallan, Perthshire on 9th July 1880.[142] Within the year, their first child, John, was born at Kilmadock, Perthshire. Robert was employed as a wood forester and the family were living in a cottage which went with the job. Two years later when a daughter Elizabeth was born, the family were still living in a forestry cottage at Kilmadock, but by the time their third child Mary, was born in 1885, the family were living in John Brown's Public House in Gargunnock. A third daughter, Helen, was born in Brown's Pub in 1888.[143]

John Brown's second son also called John, was born in 1836. By 1871 John was a 35 year old Master Blacksmith at his own Smithy at Dasherhead on the Stirling to

Gargunnock Main Street

Another late 19th century view of the Main Street looking east. Taken around the same time as the photograph on page 66. The interesting feature in this view is the open public sewer running down the north side of the street.

Dumbarton road. In the National Census of that year he is shown as a married man, employed one man, his 25-year-old brother Alexander, and a 17-year-old apprentice, William Kennedy, born in Gargunnock.[144] His younger brother, Alexander Brown, was born in 1847. He married 26-year-old Mary Crawford, the daughter of William Crawford, grocer, and Mary Glen from Lower Bridge Street in Stirling, at a Church of Scotland ceremony in Mary's home on 11th December 1878.[145] By 1880, Alexander had taken over as Master Blacksmith at the Dasherhead Smithy. Alexander prospered at Dasherhead and in the 1881 National Census is listed as employing two men and a boy.[146] A year later in November 1882, a daughter Williamina Brown was born. The Smithy is still there today, having later become a petrol filling station and is now a tea-room and car sales establishment.

In the same Census of 1881, his father, John Brown, is listed as a 70-year-old widower and spirit dealer, living on his own in the pub. His wife, Mary Livingstone, had died seven years earlier in August 1874. In May 1884, probably much to Robert's disappointment, his father sold the property to his brother, Alexander Brown for £200.[147] Prior to the birth of Mary Brown in 1885, Robert Brown and his family moved into Gargunnock

Brown's Pub is offered for sale on 19th October 1900.

to run the Public House. Robert Brown and his family remained in the property managing the Public House on his brother's behalf for the next fifteen years or so, until Robert's own death in November 1899, aged 65.[148] His widow Mary Crawford continued to run Brown's Pub until her brother in law sold the property a year later to Mr Robert Stevenson, Minister of Gargunnock and his friend Mr Alexander Leslie Brown Douglas, Advocate, of Edinburgh.

On 27th May 1894, Alexander Brown had been ordained an Elder of Gargunnock Parish.[149] The ownership of a Public House and making profit from the evils of drink would have sat heavy on the shoulders of a man who was expected to set an example to the rest of the parishioners. An advertisement offering the property for sale appeared in the *Stirling Journal and Advertiser* on 19th October, 1900.[150] There can be little doubt that the sale of Brown's Pub and subsequent opening of the Temperance Club and Reading Rooms was discussed between the minister and Alexander Brown. Almost exactly one year after the death of his brother, the pub was sold to the Mr Stevenson and Mr Alexander Leslie Brown Douglas for the sum of £600, exactly three times the amount Alexander Brown paid his father.[151]

There appeared to have been some degree of animosity over the sale, with the trustees of the cessio estate of the late Robert Brown suing his brother Alexander for payment of 'Goodwill' for the Public House which had been carried on for many years by Robert Brown. The case was abandoned by the pursuers one week before it was due to come before the Court of Session in Edinburgh.[152] By the time of the sale the Brown family had owned the property for over thirty years. Mr Stevenson and Mr Brown Douglas concluded the legalities which gave them possession of the property on 28th November 1900. What became of Mary Crawford and her 12-year-old daughter Mary, is unknown.

Gargunnock Children

This photograph of bare footed children in the Square, Gargunnock, was taken some time between 1901 when the Guest House opened and 1910 when the Memorial Fountain was erected. The pile of crates lying beside the hedge and paraffin lamp standard, probably contain empty lemonade bottles from the Guest House. There appears to be work going on in Glenfoyle cottage, tradition has it that the cottage was so named because it was for many years the home of the manager of the nearby Glenfoyle Distillery.

The Rev Stevenson and the Guest House

The Rev. Dr. Robert Stevenson BD was a direct descendant of Andrew Simson, Minister of Dunbar in 1564. He was born in Alloa, 26th May 1861, the son of John Stevenson and Jeanie Miller. His father was a Coal Master and farmer from Lilliehill, Dunfermline. Educated at Dunfermline High School and University of St Andrews, Cambridge, BA (1884), and Edinburgh, BD (1887); he was Licensed by the Presbytery of Dunfermline in 1887; he was assistant in Galashiels and ordained a Minister 5th September 1888.[153] He arrived in Gargunnock soon afterwards replacing Mr Stark who had died at Gargunnock Railway Station of a heart attack in March 1888.[154]

Reverend Dr. Robert Stevenson B.D.

Dr Stevenson's mother Jeannie Stevenson, lived at the manse until her death in August 1908 aged 83. On 6th July 1909, aged 48, he married Agnes Jeannie Dodds the daughter of Reverend Dr James Dodds Minister of Corstorphine.[155] Deeply interested in foreign missions, he influenced many to offer themselves as missionaries and was the driving force behind the establishment of the Stirling and Dunblane Presbyterial Missionary Association. Later accompanied by his wife he conducted a personal tour of mission stations in India.[156]

As soon as the money changed hands the Public House was closed down. Within a few months the house was reopened this time as a Temperance Club and Coffee House. The co-owner, Mr Alexander Leslie Brown Douglas, an Edinburgh stockbroker, came from a very wealthy family. His parents appear to have died while he was still young. Both he and his younger sister Albinnia were brought up by their oldest sister Charlotte, who was 12 years his senior and older brother Francis 10 years his senior. The house in Moray Place, Edinburgh boasted ten servants including a butler, cook and groom.[157]

The new establishment 'The Guest House', as it was called, became a centre for the more genteel activities of reading, singing and playing musical instruments. In November 1903, the activities of the Gargunnock Reading and Recreation Club made the local newspaper, when a concert of vocal and instrumental music was held in the Guest House.

> **CONCERT,** *The members of the Reading and Recreation Club were treated to a grand concert of vocal and instrumental music in the Guest House on the evening of Tuesday last. Mr A. L. Brown Douglas occupied the chair. The programme embraced violin solos by Miss Stirling, Gargunnock House and songs by Miss Burn Murdoch, Gartincaber and Mr A. L. Brown Douglas and catchew by Mr, Mrs and the Misses Brown Douglas, Leckie House. Miss Albinia Brown Douglas played the accompaniments. The concert was greatly enjoyed by all; every performer being called upon for encore. Among those present were Capt Horton, Gargunnock House, and Rev Robert Stevenson, The Manse. The usual votes of thanks and singing the King's Anthem brought a close to a very pleasant entertainment.*[158]

The Stevenson Memorial Fountain.

Reverend Stevenson is still remembered in Gargunnock, mainly through his donation of the village Public Water Supply and the Memorial Fountain in the square. Both he and his co-owner of the Temperance Club, Mr Alexander Leslie Brown Douglas, freely gave the ground on which the Fountain stands to the village, responsibility for which once lay with the parish minister.[159]

Dr Stevenson's involvement in the water project began after a disappointing District Water Board report into the feasibility of a public water supply for the village. It concluded that the cost of the scheme would be prohibitive, both in the initial construction and the subsequent annual charge, spread within a small community.[160] It seemed therefore that the scheme should be abandoned. On hearing of this the Rev Stevenson offered to defray the costs of introducing the water. In doing so, he stated that he wished to commemorate his mother, who had lived at Gargunnock Manse for some years. The Fountain and a number of black cast iron hydrants dotted around the village are now the only the visible part of the scheme.

The project was to draw water from the Gargunnock burn high above the village and lay it into a considerable number of houses in Gargunnock and its environs. The scheme consisted of an intake weir and adjoining well in the hills. A fireclay pipe conduit led from the intake well to another well or chamber, into which the water flowed by gravitation. A cast iron pipe siphon conduit, descended to and passed along the burn to a third well or chamber. A final fireclay pipe then conveyed the water to the service tank or reservoir. The total length of the various conduits from intake to tank, was 140 yards. The tank which held 33,000 gallons, was situated 160 feet above the square of Gargunnock and 60 feet above the highest house. A cast iron main was laid into the Square and from there some distance along both main street and station road. Branch pipes were then laid along other roads. A number of lion-head pillar street hydrants were erected throughout the Village.[161]

The opening ceremony of the Stevenson Water Supply Works and Memorial Fountain, took place on Tuesday 22nd March 1910. Many people associated with the Guest House were present, including, Dr Stevenson, his wife Jeanie, Mr Brown Douglas co owner of the Guest House and one of his sisters. Unfortunately, the latter two could be any one of a number of people on the platform. *For a list of those present see identities page 75.*

At the time of the official opening the Square was thronged with villagers and dignitaries. A platform had been erected in front of the Fountain and was covered in yellow cloth. A number of the surrounding houses put out flags. Among the dignitaries were Sir Alan H. Seton Steuart of Touch and Mr and Mrs Younger MP. After various speeches, the water was turned on by Mrs Jeanie

The Water Supply and Memorial Fountain Ceremony

The opening ceremony of the Gargunnock Public Water Supply and Stevenson Memorial Fountain in March 1910. Many of the village and parish worthies were present. The young boy on the left of the photograph was John McNeil he was destined be killed during the Great War.

Stevenson, wife of the Minister. To demonstrate the pressure, a hose was attached to the main pipe, when the water was turned on, a jet of water was thrown up higher than the surrounding houses. This attracted a great cheer. The Fountain itself was unveiled by Mrs R. S. Miller, a relative of the Stevensons'. The Fountain is a heavy square erection made of Bannockburn freestone after an English design. On the raised panel in front is the following inscription:

> MCMIX – In loving memory of Jeannie Miller, widow of John Stevenson, Lilliehill, Dunfermline, the water supply of Gargunnock was given by her son, the Rev Robert Stevenson, minister of the parish, and this fountain was erected by her nephews. 'The fruit of the righteous is a tree of life' – Prov. xi, 30.

The following scriptural quotation also appears on three sides of the fountain:

> "Jesus said whosever drinketh of the water that I shall give him shall never thirst."

The Fountain was walled in and seats were placed inside the enclosure. The donors of the fountain were the late Jeannie Miller's nephews. After the ceremony the company adjourned to the nearby School House for tea and cakes and more speeches.[162] Little did the crowd realise as they posed for their picture that within four short years a war like no other before or since would transform their world creating greater changes than even the reformers of the 18th and 19th centuries could ever have imagined.

By 1910, the Guest House was thriving, selling coffee, tea and lemonade to increasing numbers of people who visited the Village during the day and in the evenings catering to the villagers who used the club for reading and social functions. The same year in which the village received its water supply, the assessors of the Inland Revenue visited every household and business premise in the country. The idea behind the survey, which could be likened to a latter day Doomsday book, was to record property details with a view to introducing a new rating system. The entry for the Guest House shows it as a building of common rubble construction under a slate roof, both in fair repair. It had running water and consisted of four rooms, a kitchen and one attic room. Also included was the garden on the opposite side of the road.[163] The remainder of the terrace which now belonged to Alexander McNair was described as rubble all round rough cast good repair, slate roof. Wash house rubble wall all round bad repair with a pan tile roof. Two storeys, 3 rooms and a kitchen, no running water. Water closet and wash house in the garden.[164]

The Guest House appeared to have thrived until 1914 and the beginning of the First World War. It then apparently began to decline, probably due to the fact that most men were away at war. Those who remained had their minds on things other than temperance. The war to end wars took its toll on Gargunnock and like almost every other community in the Empire, she sacrificed her sons. The women left behind, the mothers, wives and sweethearts organised various functions including concerts in the Village School to help raise funds to support the men at the front, all the while dreading the knock on the door which heralded the arrival of the postman with a telegram. When the war ended the Village had lost nine of her sons, six of whom were born in Gargunnock. Two Gargunnock families made the ultimate sacrifice not once but twice.[165] By the end of the Great War most of the old estates were in serious decline, with the traditional role and place of the landed families in rural society beginning to change as a less deferential society emerged from the carnage.

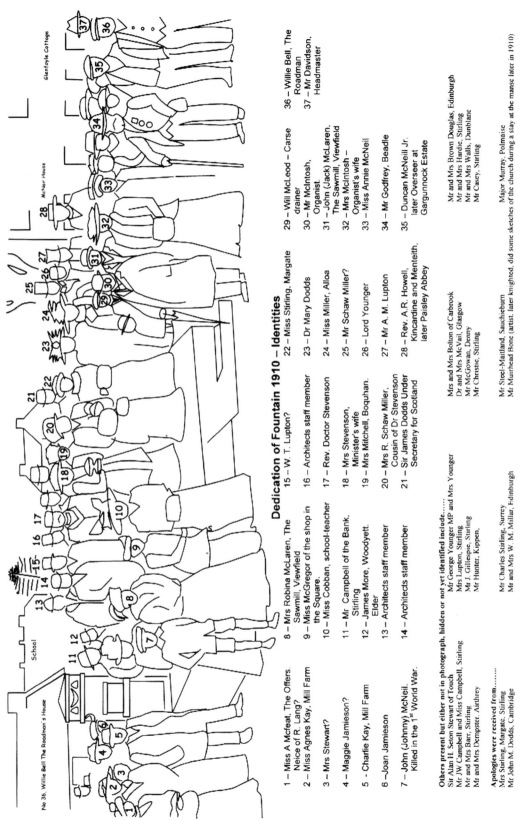

Labels on drawing: No 36. Willie Bell The Roadman's House · School · Glengoyle Cottage · McNair House

Dedication of Fountain 1910 – Identities

1 – Miss A McfFeat, The Offers.
Neice of R. Lang?
2 – Miss Agnes Kay, Mill Farm
3 – Mrs Stewart?
4 – Maggie Jamieson?
5 – Charlie Kay, Mill Farm
6 – Joan Jamieson
7 – John (Johnny) McNeil.
Killed in the 1st World War.

8 – Mrs Robina McLaren, The
Sawmill, Viewfield
9 – Miss McGregor of the shop in
the Square.
10 – Miss Cobban, school-teacher
11 – Mr Campbell of the Bank,
Stirling
12 – James More, Woodyett.
Elder
13 – Architects staff member
14 – Architects staff member

15 – W. T. Lupton?
16 – Architects staff member
17 – Rev. Doctor Stevenson
18 – Mrs Stevenson,
Minister's wife
19 – Mrs Mitchell, Boquhan.
20 – Mrs R. Schaw Miller,
Cousin of Dr Stevenson
21 – Sir James Dodds Under
Secretary for Scotland

22 – Miss Stirling, Margate
23 – Dr Mary Dodds
24 – Miss Miller, Alloa
25 – Mr Schaw Miller?
26 – Lord Younger
27 – Mr A. M. Lupton
28 – Rev. A.R. Howell,
Kincardine and Menteith,
later Paisley Abbey

29 – Will McLeod – Carse
drainer
30 – Mr McIntosh,
Organist.
31 – John (Jack) McLaren,
The Sawmill, Viewfield
32 – Mrs McIntosh –
Organist's wife
33 – Miss Annie McNeil
34 – Mr Godfrey, Beadle
35 – Duncan McNeill Jr.
later Overseer at
Gargunnock Estate

36 – Willie Bell, The
Roadman
37 – Mr Davidson,
Headmaster

Others present but either not in photograph, hidden or not yet identified include……

Sir Alan H. Seton Stewart of Touch
Mr JW Campbell and Miss Campbell, Stirling
Mr and Mrs Barr, Stirling
Mr and Mrs Dempster, Airthrey

Mr George Younger MP and Mrs Younger
Mrs Lupton, Stirling
Mr J. Gillespie, Stirling
Mr Hunter, Kippen,

Mrs and Mrs Bolton of Carbrook
Dr and Mrs McVail, Glasgow
Mr McGowan, Denny
Mr Chrstie, Stirling

Mr and Mrs Brown Douglas, Edinburgh
Mr and Mrs Hardie, Stirling
Mr and Mrs Walls, Dunblane
Mr Casey, Stirling

Major Murray, Polmaise

Apologies were received from……

Mrs Stirling, Margate. Stirling
Mr John M. Dodds, Cambridge

Mr Charles Stirling, Surrey
Mr and Mrs W. M. Millar, Edinburgh

Mr Steel-Maitland, Sauchieburn
Mr Muirhead Bone (artist, later knighted, did some sketches of the church during a stay at the manse later in 1910)

Those personalities identified in the dedication of the Memorial Fountain photograph.

For a number of years the mansion house and grounds of Stirling of Gargunnock was let to tenants who wished to live the life of a country gentleman. Francis Brown Douglas, brother of Alexander Leslie Brown Douglas, took the lease for several years during and after the Great War.[166] The Guest House closed in 1916 or 17 and lay empty for a couple of years and although the property remained in the hands of Dr Stevenson and Mr Brown Douglas, Francis Brown Douglas assumed the responsibility for the upkeep of the building while he was living at Gargunnock House, perhaps while Dr Stevenson was abroad.[167] Various tenants then occupied the house until 1927, the same year Mr Stevenson retired when it was sold.[168]

This insight into the history of the Parish and Village of Gargunnock will stop at this point. Perhaps one of the natives of the Parish will bring the story up to date with an account of the Parish and Village over the last eighty years or so. The Village in particular has seen a number of significant changes in the last eight decades. The arrival of the telephone in 1918, electric power in 1938, electric street lights in 1949 were all milestones. Gargunnock and its personalities, the parish during the Second World War and the subsequent expansion of the village after the war would all be as interesting as the history just covered.

Guest House, Gargunnock

THE GARGUNNOCK GUEST HOUSE taken about 1906. The sign above the door is offering Teas, Coffee and Lemonade. The woman in the doorway may be Mrs McQueen, she was the wife of Mr George McQueen, one time caretaker at the Guest House. The iron horse ring which can be seen to the left of the doorway is still there today.

The Gargunnock Fallen
THE GREAT WAR 1914-1918

He whom this scroll commemorates
was numbered among those who,
at the call of King and Country, left all
that was dear to them, endured hardness,
faced danger, and finally passed out of
the sight of men by the path of duty
and self sacrifice, giving up their own
lives that others might live in freedom.
Let those who come after see to it
that his name be not forgotten.

*Memorial Scroll presented to the next of kin
of the fallen.*

Private John McNeill, was born in 1897 in Gargunnock. The son of Dougal and Jessie McNeill of the Gardens, Gargunnock. John was serving with 11th Battalion The Royal Scots, when he was killed in action near Ypres, Belgium, on 12 October 1917, aged 20. He is buried in the military cemetery at Poelcappell, 10km north east of Ieper. Belgium. *(John McNeil is the boy on the left in the fountain ceremony photograph.)*

Private John More, was born in 1898 in Gargunnock. The son of John and Minnie More of Burnside, Gargunnock. John enlisted in Falkirk and was serving with the 13th Battalion The Royal Scots, when he was killed in action near Loos on 11th May 1916, aged 18. He is buried at Duds Corner Military Cemetery, near Loos, France.

Private Robert Clark, was born in Gargunnock in 1889. The son of George and Annie Clark of Bridge Haugh, Stirling. Robert enlisted in Dunblane and was serving with the 1st Battalion The Gordon Highlanders, when he died of wounds in a British field hospital in St Omar, on 27th May 1916, aged 27. He is buried at Longuenesse Military Cemetery, near St Omar, Pas de Calais, France.

Private Andrew Law, born in 1895 in Gargunnock. The son of George and Isabella Law of the Station House, Westfield, Linlithgow. Andrew was serving with the 9th Battalion The Black Watch and was killed in action at the battle of Loos, on Saturday 25th September 1915, aged 20. He is buried at Philosophe in the British Military Cemetery, near Mazingarbe, Pas de Calais, France.

Lance Corporal John Craik, was born in 1894 in Gargunnock. The son of James and Margaret Craik of Gargunnock. John enlisted in August 1915 and was serving with 11th Battalion The Argyll and Sutherland Highlanders, when he was killed in action on 23rd April 1917, near Arras, aged 23. John was a gamekeeper in Gartshore prior to the outbreak of war, and was a renowned marksman. At the time of his death, he had two brothers still serving with the army in France. He is buried at the Arras Memorial at Pas de Calais, France. Six months later the Craik family lost a second son.

Private Robert Craik, was born in Gargunnock in 1886. He was serving with the 1/7th Bn The Argyll and Sutherland Highlanders, when he was killed on the 14th October 1917. Robert was hit on the back by shrapnel from an exploding shell, during a heavy enemy bombardment. He was 31 years of age and before the war was employed with his father, in the family basket making business in Gargunnock. He is buried in Guemappe British Cemetery, Wancourt, Pas de Calais, France.

Private Robert Watson Tait, resident of Gargunnock was born in 1889. The son of John and Elizabeth Tait of Waterside House, Callender, Perthshire. Robert was serving with 1st Battalion The Cameronians (Scottish Rifles) when he was killed in action on Tuesday 29th August 1916, on the Somme, aged 27. He has no known grave, his name is inscribed on the Thiepval Memorial.

Sergeant William Baker, resident of Gargunnock, was serving with the 11th Bn The Argyll and Sutherland Highlanders, when he died of wounds on Thursday 2nd August 1917. The son of Edward Gustavus and Francis Baker of Glasgow, William was aged 38, when he succumbed to his wounds in No. 23 Casualty Clearing Station, in Belgium. Sergeant Baker was an ex regular soldier who had served 18 years with the colours, having first joined as a 14 year old boy. He fought in the South African campaign and held the Queen's Medal with four bars and the King's Medal with two bars. Sergeant Baker's father was also a regular soldier serving as a Quarter Master Sergeant in the Royal Army Medical Corps. William Baker left a young son orphaned having lost his wife the previous year. Sergeant Baker is buried at the Brandhoek New Military Cemetery, Ieper, Belgium.

Private James Don, was born at Meiklewood, son of Mr John Don, butler at Meiklewood and Mrs Margaret Don. James was killed in action on the 11th September 1916, aged 24. James was serving with the 1/7th Bn The Argyll and Sutherland Highlanders. He is buried in the Cite Bonjean Military Cemetery, Armentieres, France. Almost exactly one year later This family lost a second son. Private Alexander Don, died of wounds on Saturday 15 September 1917, aged 29. Alexander was serving with the 16th Bn The Royal Scots. A watchmaker in civilian life, he had only recently returned to the front line, having been previously invalided home with trench foot. He is buried in Tincourt Cemetery, Somme, France. This family sent four sons to the front, James, William, Connal and Alexander.

A War Memorial, designed by Sir Robert Lorrimer and inscribed with the names of the fallen, was erected in Gargunnock Kirk.

LEST WE FORGET

MINISTERS OF GARGUNNOCK 1615-1927

William Justice 1615-51. Born about 1590. Educated at Edinburgh University. Died Sept 1651.

Archibald Muschett 1652-62. Transferred to Larbert 1662.

Robert Bennett 1663-5. Transferred to Kirkintilloch.

John Edmonstone 1666-87. Deprived by Privy Council 3rd Oct 1689. Died March 1693.

George Barclay 1688-90. Covenanter. Transferred to Uphall.

Robert Campbell 1692-6. Transferred to Old Luce.

John Warden 1698-1742. Born 1671. Married Dec 1699. Died 1751.

William Warden 1743-56. Died unmarried 17th Feb 1756.

David Thompson 1758-73. Transferred from Scots Church, Amsterdam. Transferred to St Ninian's June 1773.

William Martin 1774-87. Transferred to Grayfriars, Edinburgh. 22nd Feb 1787.

James Robertson 1787-1804. Presented by Sir James Campbell of Ardkinglass. Author of the *First Statistical Account*. Transferred to South Leith Dec 1804.

George Christison 1805-09. Presented by James Eidingtoun of Gargunnock. Died 2nd June 1809.

Alexander Davidson 1810-26. Presented James Eidingtoun of Gargunnock. Transferred to Slamannan 5th Sept 1830.

Robert Buchanan 1827-30. Presented James Eidingtoun of Gargunnock. Transferred to Saltoun 22nd Apr 1830.

James Laurie 1830-43. Presented Sir F W Drummond of Hawthornden. Author of the *Second Statistical Account*. Died 9th Feb 1843.

John Stark 1844-88. Univ of Glasgow. Married 1845 Isabella Crystal in Dasherhead. Died 1888.

Robert Stevenson, D.D. 1888-1927. Univ of St Andrews, Cambridge and Edinburgh. Married 6th July 1909 Agnes Jeannie Dodds. Died 1947 at Melrose.

The Rev. John Stark, Minister of Gargunnock

The Reverend John Stark arrived in Gargunnock in 1844. Later he married into the Crystal family who at the time were the proprietors of Glenfoyle distillery. John Stark was the Parish Minister for 44 years and was one of the local dignitaries consulted by the Ordnance Survey Cartographers when they were mapping the Parish. He died suddenly at Gargunnock railway station in 1888.

VOTERS ROLL
PARISH OF GARGUNNOCK

31ST DECEMBER 1832

The following have been extracted from the Roll of Electors for the County of Stirling as at 1st December 1833. The roll can be found in the Stirling of Gargunnock Estate Papers held in Stirling Council Archives.

1. Bain, William, tenant, Dalbrain, T. lands, Dalbrain
2. Chrystal, William, tenant, Fordhead of Boquhan, T. do. Fordhead.
3. Chrystal, Robert, tenant, Parks of Boquhan or East Mains of Boquhan, T. lands, parks, or E Mains.
4. Comrie, Peter, farmer, Hill Farm of Gargunnock, T. lands Hill Farm of Gargunnock.
5. Chalmers, James, farmer, Four-Merks of Boquhan, T. do, Four-Merks Gorbals.
6. Chrystal, Andrew, farmer, Dasherhead of Gargunnock, T. lands, Dasherhead.
7. Cowbough, Henry, farmer, Redhall, T. do, Redhall.
8. Christie, Alexander, sheriff-officer, Doune, P. Houses and garden ground, Gargunnock.
9. Dunn, John, farmer, Myreton of Boquhan, T. lands, Myreton.
10. Drummond, George, tenant, Kepdarroch, Joint T. do. Kepdarroch.
11. Drummond, James, tenant, Kepdarroch, joint T. do. Kepdarroch.
12. Dunn, John, tenant, Knock of Ronald, T. do. Knock of Ronald.
13. Downie, James, of Mossend, P. do. Mosshead of Creoch.
14. Eidington, James of Gargunnock, transferred from Freeholders' Roll of 1831.
15. Ferguson, Colin, shoemaker, Gargunnock, P, houses and garden grounds Gargunnock.
16. Forrester, Samuel, tenant, Greenfoot, T. lands, Greenfoot.
17. Forrester, James, tenant, Piperland, T. do. Piperland.
18. Forrester, George, tenant, Crawtree, T. do. Crawtree.
19. Graham, David, of Meiklewood, P. do. Meiklewood.
20. Harvey, William, farmer, Byreburn, T. do. Byreburn.
21. Johnstone, Robert, farmer, Easter Culmore, tenant, lands, Easter Culmore.
22. Kay, James, contractor, Gargunnock, P. houses and ground, Gargunnock.
23. Kay, John, farmer, Gargunnock, T. lands, Glenburine.
24. Leckie, Andrew, farmer, Garrique, T. do. Garrique.
25. Lang, Robert, tenant, Beild, T. do. Upper and Nether Beild.
26. Moir, Charles Alexander, of Leckie, transferred from the Roll of Freeholders of 1831.
27. Mackison, Peter, farmer, Oldhall, T. do. lands, Oldhall.
28. Muirhead, John, do. Burnfoot, T. do. Burnfoot, Backside and Standmilane.
29. McNair, William, do. Upper Redhall, T. do. Upper Redhall.
30. McNie, John, do. Woodyet, T. do. Woodyet.
31. McEwan, William, tenant, Culbeg, T. do. Culbeg.
32. Mitchell, Matthew, do. Spittleton, T. do. Spittleton.
33. Mitchell, James, senior, grocer, Gargunnock, P. houses and ground, Gargunnock.
34. Reid, Hugh, farmer, Gargunnock, T. lands and mill, Gargunnock.
35. Richardson, Henry, tenant, Wester Culmore, T. lands , wester Culmore.

36. Robertson, James, do. Inch, T. do. Inch.
37. Shaw, John, do. Damside, T. do. Damside.
38. Taylor, George, schoolmaster, Gargunnock, P. during incumbency, house, garden, byre and glebe, Gargunnock.
39. Watt, John, tenant, Nether Patrickston, T. lands, Nether Patrickston.
40. Youll, John, grocer, Gargunnock, P. houses and ground, Gargunnock.

GARGUNNOCK FARMERS CLUB

MEMBERS

The following is a copy of the list of club members published in the *Farmer's Club Magazine* of 1920. The magazine can be found in the Stirling of Gargunnock Papers located in Stirling Council Archives.

*The names marked with an * are the Secretaries of the Club*

1794 to 1917

General John Fletcher Campbell of Boquhan, President.
James Eidington of Gargunnock
Peter Speirs of Culcreuch
Robt. Cunningham Graham of Gartmore
Robert Dunsmore of Ballindalloch
Thomas Dunsmore, yr. of Ballindalloch
Commissary McKillop, Stirling
Robert Key of Wnght's Park
George Galbraith of Blackhouse
David Forrester of Polder
George Leny of Nether Guns
Graham Leny, writer, Edinburgh
*Rev. Christopher Tait, Kincardine Manse
Captain McAlpine, Arnmore,
*John Galbraith, merchant, Kippen
Robert. Colquhoun, Touch
Cumberland Lauder, St. Ninians
John Stewart, Redhall
William Harvie, Chalmerstown
Robert. Neilson, Touch
Thomas Campbell, surgeon, Balfron
Thomas Whyte, Culcreuch Cotton Works
*Peter Gordon, Gartmore
Colonel Eidington, yr. of Gargunnock
William. Mitchell, governor, Gargunnock House
James Key, junior, Wnght's Park
William Cunningham Graham of Gartmore
Peter Graham, Aberfoyle
William Hutton wright, Gargunnock
Archibald Crawford, broker, Leith
Captain Macpherson, Lochend
Captain Graham, Duchra
Peter Currie, Livilands
James Stewart, Westwood
John Forrester, West Frew

David Erskine of Cardross	1802
Samuel Couper of Ballindalloch	1802
*Robert Patterson, Easter Frew	1803
William Christie, Boquhan	1804
John Cassels, Kepdarroch	1804
*John Leckie of Broich	1804

Robert Paterson, Mid Frew	1806
Thomas Weir, surgeon, Kippen	1806
Rev. Mr. Christison, Gargunnock Manse	1806
*Robert Banks of Craighead	1808
Provost Glass, Stirling	1809
John Muirhead, Bumfoot	1809
James Wingate, Meldrum	1810
Thomas Ord, Blair Drummond	1810
Right Honourable, The Earl of Moray	1811
James Lamb, Garden	1811
James Morrison, Blackhouse	1811
James Stirling, younger of Garden	1811
Thomas Downie of Frew	1811
James Smith, Deanston	1812
James Comrie, Gargunnock	1812
James McFarlane, Doune	1813
James Edmond of Conyhill	1813
John Robertson, Doune Castle	1813
Rev. Alex Gray, Kincardine	1813
James Sand, Cardross	1813
Archibald Lyle of Achyle	1813
John Mitchell	1813
James Walker	1813
John Cassels of Arnprior	1813
Alexander Lauder, Grahamstown	1813
Walter Zuill, Mye	1814
Alexander Mill, Gartmore	1814
William Forrester, Mid Frew	1815
Peter Robertson, Craighead	1815
William Galbraith, writer, Stirling	1815
Archibald Thomson, Powlback	1815
Henry Richardson, Culmore	1816
William Murdoch, Offers	1816
Frederick McLagan, Old Croft	1816
Robert Haldane, writer 1 Stirling	1816
John Sawers, yr of Shirgarton	1817
Henry Fletcher Campbell, Boquhan	1817
Samuel Forrester, Kerse of Leckie	1818
William. Key, Wnght's Park, Kippen	1818
John McQueen, Arnieve	1818
James Swan, Ammore, Kippen	1818
Archibald Neilson, Easter Garden	1818
Andrew Chrystal, Dasherhead	1821
Henry Home Drummond of Blair Drummond	1821
Peter McEwen, Black Dub	1823
Andrew Wingate, Bankhead	1823
John MacNie, Woodyett	1823
Major Graham of Meiklewood	1823
Robert Leckie, Settie	1824
Capt. Alex. Graham Spiers, Culcreuch	1826
Robert Dunmore Napier of Ballikinrain	1826
John Burn Murdoch of Coldoch	1827
James Cowan, Jnr, Fintry	1827
James Morrison, Clan Gregor	1827
Robert Lang, Bield of Leckie	1829
*John Patterson, Easter Frew	1829

John Doig, Easter Frew	1829
George Forrester, Crawtree	1830
Robert Chrystal, Boquhan	1832
George Paterson, Wester Frew	1832
William Murdoch Jnr, Offers	1832
William Finch, Easter Kames	1832
James Sands, jun., Cardross	1832
William Hardie, Mackeanston	1832
Rev. Dr. Gray, Kincardine Manse	1832
Thomas Murdoch, Cambusdrenny	1832
David Harvie, Arnprior	1832
David Cassels, Kepp, Arnprior	1832
John Paterson, Macoristown	1833
William Carrick, Baad	1833
James Forrester, Nether Kerse	1834
William. Forrester, Greenfoot	1835
Philip Barrington Ainslie, Factor to Lord Moray	1836
John Alexander, Little Kerse	1836
David Fogo of Row	1836
James McQueen, Arnieve	1836
Alex. Forrester, Bridge of Frew	1836
Honorable. John Stewart of Cambus Wallace	1836
John Finlayson, Cambusdrenny	1836
Charles Stirling, jnr of Gargunnock	1836
John Thomas, factor, Keir	1836
James Macfarlane, builder, Doune	1836
William Leckie Ewing of Shirgarton	1836
James Graham of Leitchton	1836
James Lucas, writer, Stirling	1837
G. Home Drummond yr. of Blair Drummond	1837
James Kay, Hill Farm, Gargunnock	1837
Robert Patterson, Carse of Cambus	1838
G.H. Binning Home, yr of Argaty	1838
Archibald Mitchell, Chalmerston	1839
Thomas Robertson, Doune Castle	1839
James Forrester, Piperland	1839
Peter Dewar, Craigniven	1839
Capt. John George Graham, R.N. of Coldoch	1839
James Finlayson	1840
Alexander. Graham, Calziemuck	1840
Alexander Watt, Patrickston	1841
David Stewart, banker, Doune	1842
John Crystal, Dasherhead	1842
S.D. Stirling of Glenbervie	1842
James Bald, Westwood	1842
John Bryce, V.S., Stirling	1843
James Chrystal, Jnr, writer, Stirling	1844
James Kay, Jnr, Hill Farm, Gargunnock	1844
Robert Paterson, Culmore	1844
James Bell, Mackeanston	1845
Alexander McLaren, Murdiston	1845
Andrew Smart, Settie, Kippen	1845
Robert Bennet, Crawfordston, Kippen	1846
William Crystal, Parks of Boquhan	1846
*Alexander Buchanan, Whitehouse	1846
James Cranston	1846

Robert Paterson, Wester Frew	1846
James McGowan, Ballanton	1846
William Graham, Middle Carse, Kippen	1847
Peter Stirling, Easter Frew	1847
John McQueen, Boquhapple	1848
William McLay, Nyaad	1848
Jas. Paterson, Stock O'Broom	1848
Alex. Wingate, Bankhead	1848
David Middleton, Mill of Torr	1849
William King, Earn	1849
John McIntyre, Woodside, Doune	1850
Oliver Graham of Meiklewood	1851
William McAlpine, Bumbank, Blair Drummond	1851
William Chrystal, Cowden	1851
*Thomas Leishman, Meiklewood	1851
John Forrester, Birkenwood	1851
William Henderson, Banks	1851
Allan Ord, Burnbank, Blair Drummond	1851
Robert Patterson, Offers	1851
Peter Stirling, Easter Frew	1851
A. Glover, Landrick Castle	1852
William Drummond, Balmuir, Ochtertyre	1852
A. Jardine of Landrick Castle	1852
R Graham Moir of Leckie	1853
John Inglis, Spittalton	1853
James Ewing, Craigniven	1854
Neil McEwen, Black Dub	1854
Peter Dewar, King's Park	1854
J.G. Turnbull, Crawtree	1854
William Kay, Little Carse, Kippen	1854
James Millar, Stirling	1854
William Jaffray, Birkenwood	1855
John S. Jack, Carrat	1860
Thomas. Murdoch, Westwood	1860
Robert Sands, Greenfoot	1861
John Lang, Bield	1861
James Grav, Birkenwood	1861
Samuel F. Bain. Inch of Leckie	1861
Thomas L. Galbraith of Blackhouse	1861
H. J. F. Campbell, yr of Boquhan	1862
James Robertson, Craighead	1862
George W. Graham of Meiklewood	1863
Captain John S. Stirling of Gargunnock	1864
William Thomson, Bumbank	1865
Alexander McGregor, Easter Culmore	1865
Alexander Monteath, writer, Stirling	1865
William Ure, Crawfordston, Kippen	1865
William Forrester of Arngibbon	1868
Thomas Carrick, Easter Cambusdrenny	1868
Sir Henry Seton Steuart, Bart., of Touch and Allanton	1868
David Dewar Shaw of Touch	1868
Charles Kay, Mill of Gargunnock	1869
Robert Downie, Knock O'Ronald	1869
John More, Fordhead	1869
William Thomson, Nyaad	1869
Rev. Wm. Wilson, Kippen Manse	1870

Alexander Ferguson, Culbeg	1870
James Jardine, Killewnan	1872
Thomas Finlayson, Cambusdrenny	1872
*Matthew C. Stark, Gargunnock Manse	1874
H. D. Erskine of Cardross	1875
Right Hon. The Earl of Moray	1876
James Sand, Milton, Doune	1876
Robert Thomson, Bumbank	1876
C.S. Drummond of Blair Drummond	1877
P.F. Connal Rowan of Meiklewood	1880
Charles Stewart, Gateside, Kippen	1880
John Paterson, Wester Frew	1880
Alexander Moir, Nether Carse	1881
Robert Kay, Mains	1881
Robert Paterson, Stock O'Broom	1881
George McGowan, Ballanton	1881
Alexander Whitelaw, Leckie House	1882
Robert Fraser, Arngomery	1883
Robert MacFarlane, Offers	1883
John Mailer, Woodyett	1883
Robert Mailer. Redhall	1883
Andrew Kay, Hillhead	1883
Robert MacFarlane, Oxhill, Buchlyvie	1884
Richard Niven, Meiklewood	1884
Captain Colin M. Dundas of Ochtertyre	1884
James Paterson. Stock O'Broom	1884
Andrew Paterson, Townhead, Kippen	1885
Robert McFeat, Offers	1885
Sir Alan Seton Steuart, Bart., of Touch and Allanton	1886
Robert C. MacFarlane, West Carse	1887
Robert Fotheringham, Southfield, Blair Drummond	1887
James Risk, Wester Culmore	1887
John Drysdale, Fairfield Farming Coy, Kippen	1888
Alastair E. Graham Moir of Leckie	1888
William McKeich, Woodend, Buchlyvie	1888
R Murdoch, Strewiebank, Kippen	1888
William McLaren, Drumore, Thornhill	1888
John Murray, Munnieston	1888
Master George Francis Connal-Rowan, Meiklewood	1888
James Gray, Birkenwood	1889
Matthew Lennox, Powblack	1889
James Strang, Knockenshannoch	1889
James McFarlane, Oxhill	1890
Sam Millar, Mill of Torr	1890
David Black, South Flanders	1890
John McNivar, Cardona	1891
Dan Paterson, Drum	1891
James Dalrymple Duncan of Woodhead	1892
Lieut Col Home Drummond of Blair Drummond	1892
John Muirhead, Briarlands	1893
James Liddell, Crawfordston	1893
Robert Bowie, Coldoch	1893
James Mitchell, Carrot	1894
James Dick, Ballanton	1894
Andrew Leckie, Fourmerk	1894
James Kerr, Culmore	1894

Robert Jackson, Mains of Boquhan	1894
James Montgomery, Polder	1894
Alexander Scoular, Middlekerse	1895
John Drysdale, Fairfield	1895
Robert Downie, Knock o' Ronald	1895
Robert M'Culloch, Myrton	1895
T. Lander, Arngomery	1896
John Paterson, West Frew	1896
Peter Matson, Boquhan	1897
John Monteath of Wright Park	1897
Peter Dewar, Amprior	1897
John Muihead, Hillhead	1898
*Colin Risk, Culmore	1899
Parlane M'Farlane, West Carse	1900
William McQueen, Shirgarton	1900
Charles Stirling of Gargunnock	1901
William Hallum, Crawfordston	1901
Stephen Mitchel, Boquhan	1902
Rev. R. Stevenson, Gargunnock	1902
Rev. J. G. Dickson, Kippen	1903
Archibald Colville, Arngomery	1903
William Galbraith of Blackhouse	1903
Thomas Syme, Kippen	1903
Stephen Mitchell yr. of Boquhan	1904
William Henderson, Woodside Hotel, Doune	1905
William Thexton, Thornhill	1906
William More, Fourmerk	1906
John Lang, Culbeg	1906
George Younger of Leckie	1906
James Lang, Bield	1907
George Paterson, Watson	1907
William McEwan, Boquhapple	1907
John Bain, Crawtree	1908
James Christie, West Carse	1909
John Mailer, Redhall	1909
William Paterson, Bield	1910
Alexander Bonthrone, Craighead	1910
Sam Bain, Mains	1910
Rev. P G Smith, Manse, Kippen	1911
James Murray, Munnieston	1912
James Gray, Crawfordston	1912
John McDougall, Knowhead	1912
Earl of Moray, Doune Lodge	1912
Capt Home Drummond Moray, Blair Drummond	1912
Capt. James Dundas, R.F.A.,Ochtertyre	1912
David Arnot, East Frew	1913
John Dunlop, Clony	1913
James Maxwell, Earland	1913
Sir Douglas A. Seton Steuart, Bart., of Touch	1914
James Kay, Mill Farm	1914
Dr. McDairmid, Oakbank	1914
John Robb Paterson, Bield	1915
James More, Woodyette	1915
James Paterson, Powblack	1916
John Syme, Middle Kerse	1917
George Paterson, West Frew	

The Square, Gargunnock

The Square, Gargunnock looking west. The sign above the Guest House door has been removed, therefore the photograph was taken some time after 1917. The single storey extension on the eastern gable of the Guest House has yet to be converted into part of the accommodation.

GARGUNNOCK PARISH PLACENAMES 1857

The following are descriptions of the locations annotated on the Ordnance Survey Map of 1860, covering Gargunnock Parish. The descriptions are extracts from the cartographer's *Name Books* and are what they saw when they visited the various locations and spoke to the owners and tenants. The accuracy of the names were checked with local dignitaries like the Lairds and Parish Minister. The *Name Books* can be found in the Scottish National Archive at West Register House in Edinburgh, under reference RH4/23/187 Book 14.

Gargunnock Village
The village is poor most of the inhabitants being labourers and no trade of any kind is done in the neighbourhood. It consists of one and two storey houses, partly thatched and partly slated. Generally in bad repair and many are ruinous. They belong to various owners. There is a curious custom in the village, a man is employed to beat a drum around the village every morning at 6am to waken the people and every evening at 9pm to let them know it is time to go to bed. When it rains the old man substitutes a tin trumpet which is anything but musical to a stranger. The drummer is supplemented by subscription and receives about two pounds per year for his services. The village contains two Churches and their Schools and Manses. There are also three public houses, a Corn and Flour Mill driven by water and a Post Office.

Kipdarroch or Kepdarroch
A neat farmhouse of one storey with good steadings of two stories high. All are slated and in good repair. Situated in the margins of the river Forth and about one mile from the village. Currently in the possession of Mr Robert Graham Moir Esq, Leckie

Piperland
A neat farmhouse and steading all of 2 storeys, slated and in very good repair. The property of Robert Graham Moir of Leckie.

Beild
A neat farmhouse and steadings all of two storeys, slated and in good repair. The property of Robert Graham Moir of Leckie.

Free Church Manse
A small plain substantial two storey building in good repair. The property of the Free Church. Built in 1846 at the west end of the village. Splendid Views.

Meiklewood Bridge
A handsome suspension bridge of one arch. It crosses the Forth on the road from Gargunnock to Kincardine. It was built twenty years ago by Col Graham of Meiklewood, but has since been sold to the Forth and Clyde Railway Co to whom it now belongs. There is a portage charge of 1d for every person crossing it and 2d for every horse.

Foot O' Green
A few cottages and a Free Church. The houses are all slated and in tolerable repair.

Rhone Well
A spring of very excellent water, but not possessing any medicinal or saintly qualities.

Dasherhead
A house and steading both of two storeys and in good repair. The property of John Stirling Esq.

Flechams
A house and steading of two storeys, slated and in good repair. The name signifies wet or marshy. The property of John Stirling.

Mains of Gargunnock
A dilapidated farm steading now used as a cottage, slated and partly in ruins. The property of John Stirling.

Meiklewood Tile Works
Several wooden sheds used for making drainage tiles, principally for the adjacent farms. The property of David Graham.

Meiklewood House
A handsome stone edifice three storeys high, slated and in good repair. The property of David Graham of Meiklewood.

Byreburn
An old steading, some straw and some slate. In a ruinous state. The property of John Stirling.

Woodyett
A farm steading, slated and in good repair. The property of David Graham of Meiklewood.

Gargunnock House
A handsome stone mansion two storeys high, slated and in good repair. The property of John Stirling of Gargunnock.

Post Office
A small one storey , thatched plain, private dwelling building. Post arrives at 12 mid day and departs at 4 p.m.

Upper Redhall
A farm steading of one storey, slated and in bad repair.

Ballochleam / Backside
Former farm steadings now in ruins.

Gallows Hill
The place where the Barons of Leckie exercised their power of Pit and Gallows.

St Colm's Glen
A small glen in which a minister once preached to Covananters.

Burntown
A few cottages all of one storey and slated. Contains a smithy and a dwelling house which was formerly a school.

Myreton
A farm steading of one storey, slated and in good repair. The property of H. F. Campbell Esq.

Fourmark
A farm steading of one storey, slated and in good repair. The property of H. F. Campbell Esq.

Auldhall

A farm steading of one storey, slated and in good repair. The property of H. F. Campbell Esq.

Glenorgue

Cottages and a wright's shop all of one storey, slated and in good repair.

Dasher Bridge

A stone bridge of one arch crossing the Boquhan stream. Takes its name from a Mill which once stood nearby.

School House

A substantial stone building and schoolmaster's house attached. Of one storey, slated and in good repair. A government grant of £15 to the master the remainder being paid by the heritors. Average attendance 50.

Manse

A commodious and comfortable house of two stories, slated and in good repair. It was built around 1750. The glebe is about 7 acres.

Mains of Boquhan

A neat, good, substantial farmhouse and steading all of one storey, slated and in very good repair. The property of Henry Fletcher Campbell.

Leckie

A plain substantial stone building of 1, 2 and 3 storeys high. Slated and in good repair. Occupied by the servants of Mr Moir. West of but adjacent to Leckie Mansion. Built over 3 differing periods the original erection date is unknown. On an old, disused, nameless, stone bridge which stands nearby at the Mill of Leckie, is the following inscription in stone *Ex Benevolentia ob Salutem* ' (Out of good will for safety).

Leckie

A large mansion in the old Scottish Baronial style.

Fordhead

A compact farmhouse and steading of one storey, slated and in very good repair. Situated against the Ford of Frew from which it takes its name.

Boquhan

A substantial mansion partly one and partly two stories high. Built over differing periods it has two un-ornamented fronts, one looking south, the other north. The greater part of the ornamental grounds with garden are in the parish of Kippen immediately across the Burn of Boquhan which forms the parish boundary. The park grounds are large with fine old oak trees. It is the property and residence of Mr Henry Fletcher Campbell Esq.

Lady's Well

Spring well within the gardens of Boquhan house. It received its name from a lady of the house who caused it to be made.

Inch

A small well laid out farmhouse and steading, all of two storeys and in excellent repair. The property of Mr Robert Graham Moir of Leckie.

Culmore Cottage

A small one storey house with small garden attached. Occupied by a farm servant.

Slated and going to ruin, it will soon be taken down. The property of Mr Robert Graham Moir of Leckie.

East Culmore
A plain substantial farmhouse and steading, the later of two storeys. Only the former is slated, but all is in good repair. The property of Mr Robert Graham Moir of Leckie.

West Culmore
Plain farmhouse and steading. All two storeys, slated and in good repair. The property of Mr Robert Graham Moir of Leckie.

Netherkerse
A farmhouse and steading, two storeys high, slated and in good repair. The property of Mr Robert Graham Moir of Leckie.

Patrickstown
A farmhouse and steading of one and two storeys high, slated, in only middling repair. The property of Mr Robert Graham Moir of Leckie.

Culbeg
Plain farmhouse and steading of one and two storeys high. Slated and in tolerable repair. The property of Mr Robert Graham Moir of Leckie.

Ford of Frew
The Forth at this point is very shallow. In summer it can easily be crossed dry. Until the present bridge was built it was the only place at which horses and carts could cross for miles either up or down the river. The banks on each side are low and slope to the water's edge. There is hard footing throughout the river, the bed being of sand and shingle and no rocks. Mr Campbell states that he has never heard of the ford being fortified to protect it on either side. He had heard that some of his predecessors had placed some few cannon on the Gargunnock side, but no fortifications.

Lady Betty's Well
A small spring rising from under a rock like the mouth of a drain and having no appearance of a well. It takes its name (Betty) from an old woman who lived adjacent some two hundred years ago. The are no traditions or antiquity connected with it, simply an old woman's well. It is well known in the neighbourhood.

Bridge of Otters
Name applied to what is only a ford. It is supposed to have been made by Sir William Wallace and was never anything other than a leap of stones between the banks, over which was laid some logs. It was used by natives of the parish until the building of the suspension bridge for carting peat from Kincardine Moss.

Free Church School
A one storey building, tiled and in bad repair. There is a government grant of £21 10s to the master and £5 for a pupil teacher. The remainder of the salary is paid from funds. The average attendance is 45

Gargunnock Village 1860

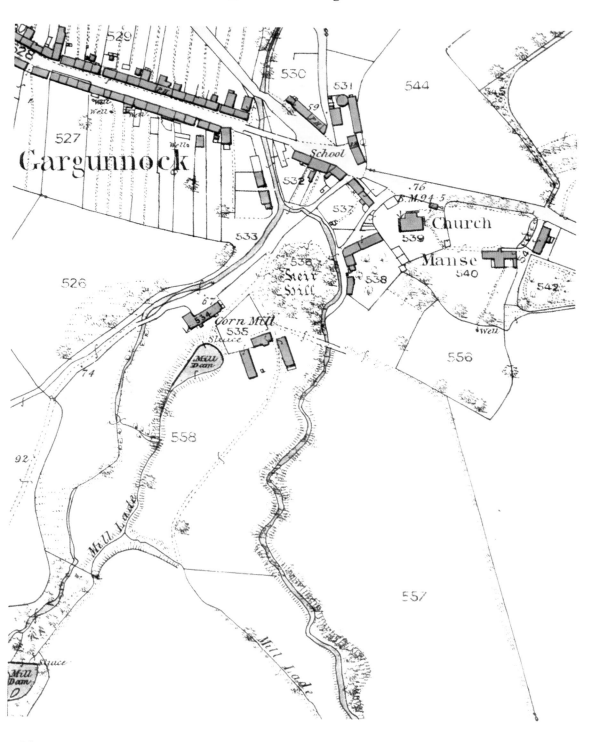

This portion of the 1860 Ordnance Survey 25" map of Gargunnock, shows the individual houses with their long narrow gardens, some with private wells. The feus have changed very little from the original areas. Unfortunately, as with Roy's Map, the village has fallen on the very edge of a map sheet.

Summary of original and early feuars of Gargunnock Village

NAME	DATE	FEU	LOCATION
David, Thomas & John Birrell	1726	½ Acre	Either side of and including the Inn on the north side of the Main St. A plot across Leckie Rd
James Adam	1726	½ Acre	West of Birrell Feu
Andrew & John Menzies	1726	¼ Acre	West of Adam's Feu
Jonathan & John Draper	1728	½ Acre	West of Menzie's Feu
James & Robert Miller	1733	½ Acre	West of Draper Feu
Archibald Stirling	1733	½ Acre	West of Miller Feu
David Findlayson	1733	¼ Acre	West of Stirling Feu
John Findlayson	1733	¼ Acre	West of Findlayson Feu
John Davidson	1733	½ Acre	Area behind current village shop
John Kay	1733	¼ Acre	West of Davidson Feu now road to McNeil Crescent
George Birrell	1733	½ Acre	West of Davidson Feu
Alexander Hardie	1734	½ Acre	West of Birrell Feu
Thomas Harvie	1740	2 Acres	West of Hardie Feu
David Graham	1760	½ Acre	Area of new cemetery (Duke St)
Robert Yool	1772	2 Acres	Area to south of Foot O' Green Cottage and behind Church Hall
Isabelle & Margt Harvie	1772	½ Acre	East of U.F.C Manse
Hugh & Archbald Wright	1772	½ Acre	East of Harvie Feu
Robert & Andrew Taylor	1772	½ Acre	East of Wright Feu
Wm Wright & Charles Freedland	1772	½ Acre	East of Taylor Feu
Archibald Stirling	1772	½ Acre	East of Wright & Freedland Feu
George Patterson	1772	½ Acre	East of Stirling Feu
John Smith	1772	½ Acre	East of Patterson Feu
John Headrick	1772	2 Acres	East of Smith Feu
James McNair	1777	1 Acre	Around the 3 sides (N, S, E) of the Square
James Mitchell	1779	2 Acres	Area to south of Rev Patterson Feu
Rev Patterson & Heritors	1783	1 Acre	Area to the west of U.F.C. Manse

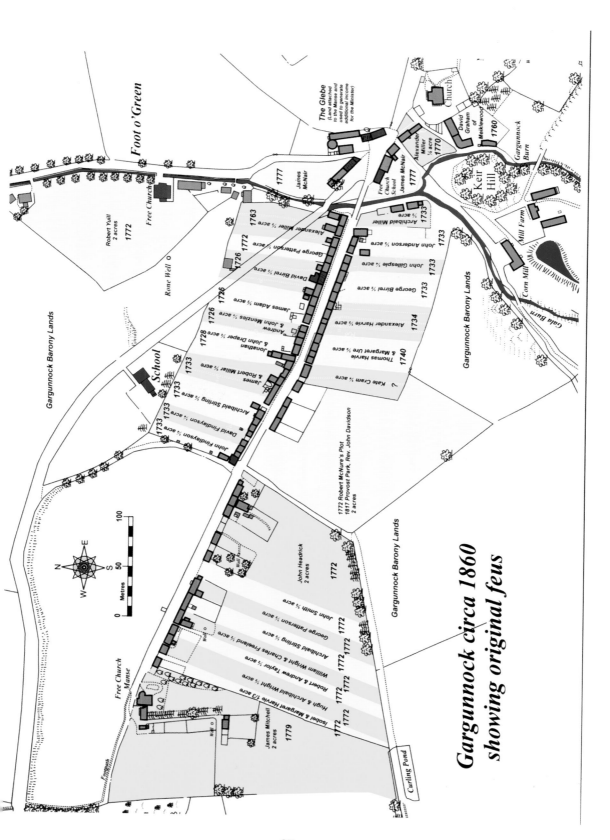

Gargunnock circa 1860
showing original feus

Foot o'Green

Robert Yuill
2 acres
1772

Free Church

Rome Well ○

Gargunnock Barony Lands

School
1733
1733

N
W E
S

Metres
0 50 100

Free Church
Manse

Footpath

James Mitchell
2 acres
1779

Curling Pond

John Findlayson ½ acre
1733

David Findlayson ½ acre
1733

James & Robert Miller ½ acre
1733

Jonathan & John Draper ½ acre
1728

Andrew & John Menzies ½ acre
1726

James Adam ½ acre
1726

David Birrel ½ acre
1726 1772

George Patterson ½ acre
1763

Alexander Miller ½ acre

James McNair
1777

Archibald Stirling ½ acre

Well ○

Hugh & Archibald Harvie 1/3 acre
1772

Isobel & Margaret Harvie 1/3 acre
1772

Robert & Andrew Taylor ½ acre
1772

William Wright & Archibald Wright ½ acre
1772

Archibald Stirling ½ acre
1772

George Patterson ½ acre
1772

Charles Freeland ½ acre
1772

John Smith ½ acre
1772

John Headrick
2 acres
1772

Well ○

1772 Robert McNure's Plot
1817 Provost Park, Rev. John Davidson
2 acres

Gargunnock Barony Lands

Kate Cram ½ acre
?

Thomas Harvie
& Margaret Ure ½ acre
1740

Alexander Harvie ½ acre
1734

George Birrel ½ acre
1733

John Gillespie ½ acre
1733

John Anderson ½ acre
1733

Free
Church
School

James McNair
1777

Archibald Miller ½ acre
1733

Alexander
Miller
¼ acre
1770

David
Graham
of
Meiklewood
1760

Church

Gargunnock
Burn

Keir
Hill

Mill Farm

Corn Mill

Gala Burn

Gargunnock Barony Lands

The Glebe
(Land attached
to the Manse and
used to generate
additional income
for the Minister)

Appendix VIII – GARGUNNOCK PARISH NATIONAL CENSUS RETURN 1881

Gargunnock Village

NAME	RELATION	MAR	AGE	OCCUPATION	BIRTHPLACE
John Travis	Head	M	29	Spale basket maker (J/man)	England
Margaret Travis	Wife	M	28	Basket maker's wife	Kirkcudbright, Kirkcudbrightshire
Frank Donald	Boarder	U	22	Spale basket maker (J/Man)	England
James Craik	Boarder	U	20	Spale basket maker	Gatehouse, Kirkcudbrightshire
George McQueen	Head	M	36	Labourer at Distillery	Kippen, Stirlingshire
Jessie McQueen	Wife	M	33	Labourer's wife	Kippen, Stirlingshire
George McQueen	Son		7	Scholar	Gargunnock, Stirlingshire
Isabella McQueen	Dau		6	Scholar	Gargunnock, Stirlingshire
Samuel McQueen	Son		7m		Gargunnock, Stirlingshire
George McQueen	Father	W	75	Retired farmer	Kincardine, Perthshire
Margaret McQueen	Sister	M	46	Gardener's wife	Kincardine, Perthshire
John Brown	Head	W	70	Publican	St Ninian's, Stirlingshire
Thomas Travis	Head	M	32	Spale basket maker (Master)	England
Jane Travis	Wife	M	34	Spale basket maker's wife	Edinburgh
Robert Travis	Son		9	Scholar	Gargunnock, Stirlingshire
Mary Travis	Dau		6	Scholar	Gargunnock, Stirlingshire
John Travis	Son		5	Scholar	Gargunnock, Stirlingshire
Janet Travis	Dau		3		Gargunnock, Stirlingshire
James	Son		1		Gargunnock, Stirlingshire
Thomas	Son		2m		Gargunnock, Stirlingshire
John McLaughlan	Head	M	60	Agricultural labourer	Stranraer, Wigtonshire.
Christina McLaughlan	Wife	M	60	Labourer's wife	Gargunnock, Stirlingshire
John McLaughlan	Son	U	30	Railway Labourer	Gargunnock, Stirlingshire
William McLaughlan	Son	U	22	Game Keeper	Gargunnock, Stirlingshire
John McLaughlan	G/Son		8	Scholar	Gargunnock, Stirlingshire
Joseph Trotter	Head	M	38	Spale basket maker (J/Man)	England
Margaret Trotter	Wife	M	35	Spale basket maker's wife	England
Ann Trotter	Dau		13	Scholar	England

Name	Relation	Status	Age	Occupation	Birthplace
Robert Trotter	Son		11	Scholar	Gatehouse, Kirkcudbrightshire
Ellen A Trotter	Dau		6	Scholar	England
Joseph	Son		3		England
Henry	Son		1m		England
William Ferguson	Head	M	27	Gardener's labourer	St Ninian's, Stirlingshire
Isabella Ferguson	Wife	M	24	Labourer's wife	Gargunnock, Stirlingshire
Peter Ferguson	Son		4		Gargunnock, Stirlingshire
Helen Ferguson	Dau		3		Gargunnock, Stirlingshire
Robert Ferguson	Son		1		Gargunnock, Stirlingshire
John Muirhead	Boarder	U	21	Joiner (J/Man)	Coatbridge, Lanarkshire
Robert Kennedy	Head	M	56	Agricultural labourer	Blackford, Perthshire
Helen Kennedy	Wife	M	53	Labourer's wife	Kippen, Stirlingshire
John Wm Kennedy	G/Son		3m		Edinburgh
Christina Fullton	Head	U	44	Former laundress	Gargunnock, Stirlingshire
Ramsey Borthwick	Head	M	30	Manager of Distillery	Dalmeny, Linlithgowshire
Janet Borthwick	Wife	M	33	Manager's wife	Uphall, Linlithgowshire
Janet Borthwick	Dau		7	Scholar	Kirkliston, Linlithgowshire
Hugh Borthwick	Son		5	Scholar	Kirkliston, Linlithgowshire
John Borthwick	Son		2	(Blind)	Bo'Ness, Linlithgowshire
Janet Mitchell	Head	U	45	Grocer	Gargunnock, Stirlingshire
Mary Mitchell	Dau	U	24	Former domestic servant	Gargunnock, Stirlingshire
Myles Newby	Head	M	25	Spale basket maker (J/Man)	England
Marion Newby	Wife	M	22	Spale basket maker's wife	England
Henry Dodgson	Boarder	U	20	Spale basket maker (J/Man)	England
Andrew McClure	Head	M	30	Painter (J/Man)	Paisley, Renfrewshire
Marion McClure	Wife	M	29	Painter's wife	Paisley, Renfrewshire
Janet McClure	Dau		10m		Glasgow, Lanarkshire
George Ogilvie	Head	W	73	Retired engineer	Longforgan, Perthshire
Elizabeth Patterson	Dau	M	32	Mason contractor's wife	Duntocher, Dumbartonshire
Robert Patterson	Son in Law	M	40	Mason contractor	Irongray Rd, Kirkcudbright
Annie Patterson	G/Dau		8	Scholar	Duntocher, Dumbartonshire
John Patterson	G/Son		7	Scholar	Glasgow, Lanarkshire

Name	Relation	Status	Age	Occupation	Birthplace
George Patterson	G/son		4		Glasgow, Lanarkshire
Lydia Patterson	G/Dau		2		Gargunnock, Stirlingshire
James Wright	Head	M	60	Mason (Master)	Gargunnock, Stirlingshire
Ann Wright	Sister	U	58	Former laundress	Gargunnock, Stirlingshire
Ellen Sinclair	Head	U	58	Washer woman	Gargunnock, Stirlingshire
Allan Beaton	G/Son		10	Scholar	Gargunnock, Stirlingshire
Jane Christie	G/Dau		7	Scholar	Gargunnock, Stirlingshire
Elizabeth Galbraith	Head	W	46	Stocking knitter	Gargunnock, Stirlingshire
William Galbraith	Son		14	Agricultural labourer	Gargunnock, Stirlingshire
John McGregor	Boarder		14	Painter (Apprentice)	Fintry, Stirlingshire.
Peter Binnie	Head	M	58	Grocer	Denny, Stirlingshire
Janet Binnie	Wife	M	50	Grocer's wife	Port of Menteith, Stirlingshire
Annie Moir	Niece	U	17	Grocer's assistant	Drymen, Stirlingshire
John McConnell	Head	M	40	Excise Officer Inland Revenue	Aldowrie, Inverness-shire
Jane Orr McConnell	Wife	M	28	Excise Office's wife	Strathaven, Lanarkshire
Maggie McConnell	Dau		3		Glasgow, Lanarkshire
John McConnell	Son		2		Gargunnock, Stirlingshire
Robert McConnell	Son		7m		Gargunnock, Stirlingshire
Margaret B Fleming	Mother in Law	W	56	Annuitant	Strathavon, Lanarkshire
Annie Fergusson	Serv		14	General domestic servant	Stirling, Stirlingshire
Helen Corran	Head	M	45	Lodging housekeeper	Ireland
Thomas Carrigan	Son	U	18	Carter	Gargunnock, Stirlingshire
John McCormack	Lodger	U	74	Road labourer	Ireland
Thomas McKnight	Lodger	U	41	Agricultural labourer	Ireland
James Cumming	Lodger	U	50	Agricultural labourer	Cullen, Ayrshire.
Jessie McDonals	Lodger	W	60	Dressmaker	Glasgow, Lanarkshire
James Miller	Lodger	M	31	Licensed hawker	Glasgow, Lanarkshire
Ann Miller	Lodger	M	40	Hawker's wife	Glasgow, Lanarkshire
John Stewart	Lodger	M	26	Licensed hawker	Mullen, Perthshire
Mary Stewart	Lodger	M	23	Hawker's wife	Monkland, Lanarkshire
James Stewart	Lodger		6m		Ballater, Aberdeenshire
Jane Lang	Head	U	66	Goes messages (Pauper)(Imbecile)	Gargunnock, Stirlingshire

Name	Relation	Condition	Age	Occupation	Birthplace
Ann Patterson	Head	U	82	Former outdoor Worker (Pauper)	Gargunnock, Stirlingshire
Thomas Clerk	Head	M	68	Spale basket maker (J/Man)	England
Mary Ann Clerk	Wife	M	46	Spale basket maker's wife	Glasgow, Lanarkshire
William Clerk	Son	U	19	Agricultural labourer	Greenock, Renfrewshire
Mary Ann Clerk	Dau		12	Scholar	Glasgow, Lanarkshire
Hugh Clerk	Son		10	Scholar	Gatehouse, Kirkcudbrightshire
James Clerk	Son		7	Scholar	England
Elizabeth McLeod	Head	W	89	Stocking knitter	Gargunnock, Stirlingshire
Robert McLeod	Head	U	48	Agricultural labourer	Gargunnock, Stirlingshire
William McLeod	Head	U	45	Agricultural labourer	Gargunnock, Stirlingshire
Mary McLeod	Dau	U	43	General servant	Gargunnock, Stirlingshire
David Dobbie	G/Son	U	20	Gardener (Apprentice)	Gargunnock, Stirlingshire
John C McDonald	Head	M	51	Agricultural labourer	Fintry, Stirlingshire
Janet McDonald	Wife	M	57	Labourer's wife	Airth, Stirlingshire
Janet McDonald	Dau	U	29	Agricultural labourer	Gargunnock, Stirlingshire
Agnes McDonald	Dau	U	22	Farm servant	Gargunnock, Stirlingshire
William McDonald	Son	U	19	Labourer at Distillery	Gargunnock, Stirlingshire
Malcolm McGregor	G/Son		11	Scholar	Gargunnock, Stirlingshire
William Lemmon	G/Son		10	Scholar	Gargunnock, Stirlingshire
Andrew McGregor	G/Son		9	Scholar	Gargunnock, Stirlingshire
Margaret McDonald	G/Dau		4		Gargunnock, Stirlingshire
Janet L McDonald	G/Dau		2		Gargunnock, Stirlingshire
John McDonald	G/Son		4m		Gargunnock, Stirlingshire
Janet Martin	Head	W	81	Stocking knitter	Port Of Monteith, Perthshire
James Baxter	Head	M	33	Labourer at Distillery	Denny, Stirlingshire
Christina Baxter	Wife	M	35	Labourer's wife	Denny, Stirlingshire
Robert Baxter	Son		7	Scholar	Gargunnock, Stirlingshire
Jane Baxter	Dau		5		Gargunnock, Stirlingshire
John Baxter	Son		3		Gargunnock, Stirlingshire
Archibald Abercrombie	Head	M	65	Road labourer	Gargunnock, Stirlingshire
Catherine Abercrombie	Wife	M	54	Labourer's wife	Glenorchy, Argyll

Name	Relation	Status	Age	Occupation	Birthplace
William Stewart	Head	M	45	General labourer	Aberfoyle, Perthshire
Janet Stewart	Wife	M	47	Labourer's wife	Gargunnock, Stirlingshire
William Bell	Head	M	31	Railway labourer	Kincardine, Perthshire
Christina Bell	Wife	M	28	Labourer's wife	Stenhousemuir, Stirlingshire
Margaret Bell	Dau		7	Scholar	Gargunnock, Stirlingshire
James Bell	Son		5		Gargunnock, Stirlingshire
William Bell	Son		3		Gargunnock, Stirlingshire
Robert Bell	Son		1		Gargunnock, Stirlingshire
Margaret Doig	Head	U	68	Agricultural labourer	Gargunnock, Stirlingshire
John Mitchell	Head	M	59	Agricultural labourer	Gargunnock, Stirlingshire
Christina Mitchell	Wife	M	37	Labourer's wife	Alloa, Clackmannanshire.
Peter Mitchell	Son		13	Scholar	Gargunnock, Stirlingshire
Christina Mitchell	Dau		10	Scholar	Gargunnock, Stirlingshire
John Mitchell	Son		9	Scholar	Gargunnock, Stirlingshire
Janet Mitchell	Dau		5	Scholar	Gargunnock, Stirlingshire
William Mitchell	Head	U	68	Shoemaker (Master)	Gargunnock, Stirlingshire
William Mitchell	Nephew		6	Scholar	Gargunnock, Stirlingshire
Neil Livingston	Boarder	M	56	Agricultural labourer	Kincardine, Perthshire
Margaret Livingston	Boarder	M	60	Labourer's wife	Gargunnock, Stirlingshire
Alexander Robertson	Head	W	62	Retired farmer	Balquidder, Perthshire
Robert Marshall	Son in Law	M	32	Agricultural labourer	Linlithgow
Elizabeth Marshall	Dau	M	26	Labourer's wife	Gargunnock, Stirlingshire
Edward Marshall	G/Son		2		Gargunnock, Stirlingshire
Alexander Marshall	G/Son		3m		Gargunnock, Stirlingshire
William McIsaac	Head	M	60	Tailor (Master)	Gargunnock, Stirlingshire
Mary McIsaaac	Wife	M	60	Tailor's wife	Rothesay, Bute
Margaret McPherson	Head	W	55	Dressmaker	Glasgow, Lanarkshire
Alexander Connell	Head	U	62	Agricultural labourer	Gargunnock, Stirlingshire
Margaret Stirling	Head	U	68	Dairy & Land 16 Acres arable	Gargunnock, Stirlingshire

Name	Relationship	Status	Age	Occupation	Birthplace
Mary Stirling	Sister	U	65	Dairy maid	Gargunnock, Stirlingshire
Robert Malcolm	Head	M	78	Agricultural labourer (Deaf)	Alloa, Clackmannanshire
Margaret Malcolm	Wife	M	76	Labourer's wife	Port of Monteith, Perthshire
Grace Wilson	G/Dau	U	15	General domestic servant	Glasgow, Lanarkshire
Robert Malcolm	G/Son		6	Scholar	Glasgow, Lanarkshire
Eliza Johnstone	Head	U	50	Dressmaker	Glasgow, Lanarkshire
Jane Campbell	Head (Wife)	M	33	Chief Constable's wife	Bandrey, Lanarkshire
Jane Campbell	Dau		4		Stirling, Stirlingshire
Helen Campbell	Dau		2		Stirling, Stirlingshire
James Livingstone	Head	M	26	Joiner (J/Man)	Gargunnock, Stirlingshire
Janet Livingstone	Wife	M	23	Joiner's wife	Balfron, Stirlingshire
Margaret Livingstone	Dau		4		Gargunnock, Stirlingshire
Neil Livingstone	Son		2		Gargunnock, Stirlingshire
Daniel Livingstone	Son		5m		Gargunnock, Stirlingshire
Margaret Forsyth	Head	W	69	Annuitant	Gargunnock, Stirlingshire
Isabella McGregor	G/Niece	U	13	Domestic servant	St Ninian's, Stirlingshire
Christina Dunlop	Head	W	66	Agricultural labourer's widow	Denny, Stirlingshire
Daniel McGregor	Son in Law	W	50	Railway labourer	Aberfoyle, Perthshire
John Morrison	Lodger	M	29	Plumber (J/Man)	Cumbernauld, Dumbartonshire
John Turnbull	Lodger	U	27	Plumber (J/Man)	Australia
Janet McNab	Head	U	56	Former domestic servant (Pauper)	Gargunnock, Stirlingshire
Jane Miller	Head	U	45	Former housemaid (Pauper)	Gargunnock, Stirlingshire
Jane Miller	Dau		12	Scholar	Newington, Edinburgh
John McGlashan	Boarder		53	General labourer (Imbecile)	Gargunnock, Stirling
Margaret Stevenson	Head	W	73	Housekeeper	Gargunnock, Stirlingshire
John Stevenson	G/Son		11	Scholar	Gargunnock, Stirlingshire
Mary Miller	Head	W	60	Housekeeper	Port of Monteith, Perthshire
Margaret Kellie	Sister	W	68	Stocking knitter	Port of Monteith, Perthshire
Janet McArthur	Head	W	76	Grocer	Gargunnock, Stirlingshire
John Patterson	Head	M	63	Retired shoemaker	Gargunnock, Stirlingshire

Name	Relation	Status	Age	Occupation	Birthplace
Mary Patterson	Wife	M	67	Shoemaker's wife	Gargunnock, Stirlingshire
Jane Patterson	Dau	U	22	Domestic servant	Gargunnock, Stirlingshire
William R Hamblin	Lodger	U	24	Excise Officer Inland Revenue	England
John Draper	Head	M	77	Agricultural labourer	Bridge of Allan, Stirlingshire
Mary Draper	Wife	m	72	Labourer's wife	Gargunnock, Stirlingshire
Catherine Jenkins	Head	W	75	Agricultural labourer's widow	Kincardine, Perthshire
Peter Jenkins	G/Son		14	General labourer	Stirling, Stirlingshire
Mary Casson	G/Dau		7	Scholar	Gargunnock, Stirlingshire
William Spence	Great G/Son		3		Stirling, Stirlingshire
Helen Smeaton	Head	W	75	Agricultural labourer's widow	Gargunnock, Stirlingshire
Alexander Robertson	Head	M	21	Gardener's labourer	Gargunnock, Stirlingshire
Agnes Robertson	Wife	M	21	Labourer's wife	Torphichon, Linlithgowshire
James Christie	Head	M	85	Retired gardener	England
Margaret Christie	Wife	M	78	Gardener's wife	Gargunnock, Stirlingshire
Clementina Christie	Dau	U	35	Housekeeper	Kilmadock, Perthshire
John Jenkins	Head	W	48	Gardener's labourer	Gargunnock, Stirlingshire
Thomas Rorie	Head	M	37	Distillery labourer	Methven, Perthshire
Isabella Rorie	Wife	M	28	Labourer's wife	Kilmadock, Perthshire
Isabella Rorie	Dau		11	Scholar	Port of Monteith, Perthshire
Janet Rorie	Dau		9	Scholar	Gargunnock, Stirlingshire
Margaret Rorie	Dau		6	Scholar	Gargunnock, Stirlingshire
William Rorie	Son		4		Gargunnock, Stirlingshire
Barbara Rorie	Dau		3		Gargunnock, Stirlingshire
Thomas Rorie	Son		10m		Gargunnock, Stirlingshire
David Taylor	Head	M	57	Former railway labourer	Kippen, Stirlingshire
Mary Taylor	Wife	M	54	Former railway labourer's wife.	Gargunnock, Stirlingshire
Maggie Jane Taylor	Dau	U	17	Dressmaker	Gargunnock, Stirlingshire
Alexander Taylor	Son		11	Scholar	Gargunnock, Stirlingshire
William McIntyre	Lodger	U	22	Joiner (J/Man)	New Monkland, Lanarkshire
Robert Mitchell	Head	U	75	Retired farmer	Gargunnock, Stirlingshire
Jean McIndoe	Servant	U	45	Cook (Gen Servant)	Gargunnock, Stirlingshire

Name	Relation	Condition	Age	Occupation	Birthplace
Jane Yuile	Head	U	57	Grocer	Gargunnock, Stirlingshire
John McClennan	Lodger	U	31	Missionary of the Free Church	Glen Urquhart, Inverness
Sarah Cowbrough	Head	W	38	Spirit Dealer	Kilmaurs, Ayrshire
Janet Cowbrough	Dau		13	Scholar	Gargunnock, Stirlingshire
William Cowbourgh	Son		11	Scholar	Gargunnock, Stirlingshire
George Cowbrough	Son		7	Scholar	Gargunnock, Stirlingshire
Janet Connal	Head	U	74	Retired agricultural labourer	Gargunnock, Stirlingshire
Robert Bennet	Head	M	49	Railway labourer	Beath, Kinross
Margaret Bennet	Wife	M	50	Railway labourer's wife	St Ninian's, Stirlingshire
Margaret Bennet	Dau	U	16	Dressmaker (Apprentice)	Gargunnock, Stirlingshire
Isabella Bennet	Dau		10	Scholar	Gargunnock, Stirlingshire
William Bennet	Son		7	Scholar	Gargunnock, Stirlingshire
Francis McNab	Head	W	79	Agricultural labourer	Killin, Perthshire
James Rorie	Head	M	32	Railway labourer	Methven, Perthshire
Janet Rorie	Wife	M	35	Railway labourer's wife	Kincardine, Perthshire
Ann Rorie	Dau		6	Scholar	Gargunnock, Stirlingshire
Janet Rorie	Dau		4		Gargunnock, Stirlingshire
David Rorie	Son		1		Gargunnock, Stirlingshire
Robert Anderson	Head	U	64	Retired farmer	St Ninian's, Stirlingshire
Catherine Anderson	Sister	U	71	Housekeeper	St Ninian's, Stirlingshire
Janet Kennedy	Head	U	73	Outdoor worker (Pauper)	Gargunnock, Stirlingshire

The Manse

Name	Relation	Condition	Age	Occupation	Birthplace
John Stark	Head	W	69	Minister of Gargunnock	London, England
Andrew Crystal Stark	Son	U	31	Mercantile clerk	Gargunnock, Stirlingshire
John Stark	Son	U	25	Insurance clerk	Gargunnock, Stirlingshire
Jane Stark	Dau	U	29	Minister's daughter	Gargunnock, Stirlingshire
Margaret Brown	Serv	U	20	Cook domestic servant	Perth, Perthshire
Elizabeth Brown	Serv	U	16	Housemaid	Perth, Perthshire

Mill Farmhouse

Name	Relation	Status	Age	Occupation	Birthplace
Charles Kay	Head	M	44	Farmer of 100 Acres arable. Employing 2 men,1 girl.	Gargunnock, Stirlingshire
Margaret Kay	Wife	M	28	Farmer's wife	Slamanan, Stirlingshire
Agnes Gray Kay	Dau		1		Gargunnock, Stirlingshire
James Kay	Son		3m		Gargunnock, Stirlingshire
John Coyne	Serv	U	19	Farm Servant	Kilmadock, Perthshire
Alexander McDonald	Serv	U	17	Farm Servant	Gargunnock, Stirlingshire
Jessie Mathison	Serv	U	17	General domestic servant	Glasgow, Lanarkshire

Dasherhead Farmhouse

Name	Relation	Status	Age	Occupation	Birthplace
Jane Lang	Head	W	59	Farmer of 103 Acres arable employing 2 men (Farm Irrigation)	Gargunnock, Stirlingshire
Margaret Bell Lang	Dau	U	29	Farmer's daughter	Port of Menteith, Perthshire
Anna Murdoch Lang	Dau	U	27	Farmer's daughter	Port of Menteith, Perthshire
Isabella Lang	Dau	U	25	Farmer's daughter	Port of Menteith, Perthshire
Jane Lang	Dau	U	23	Farmer's daughter	Port of Menteith, Perthshire
Robina Lang	Dau	U	19	Farmer's daughter	Port of Menteith, Perthshire
Georgina Lang	Dau	U	18	Farmer's daughter	Port of Menteith, Perthshire
John Lang	Son	U	18	Farmer's son	Port of Menteith, Perthshire
Robert Lang	Son	U	16	Farmer's son	Gargunnock, Stirlingshire
Ann Watt	Aunt	W	75	Farmer's widow	Kippen, Stirlingshire
James Carr	Serv	U	22	Farm servant	St Ninian's, Stirlingshire
James Stark	Serv	U	21	Farm servant	Glasgow, Lanarkshire

Gargunnock Smithy House

Name	Relation	Status	Age	Occupation	Birthplace
Alexander Brown	Head	M	33	Master blacksmith employing 2 men, 1 boy	Kincardine, Perthshire
Mary Brown	Wife	M	27	Blacksmith's wife	Stirling, Stirlingshire
Robert Brown	Nephew	U	25	Blacksmith	Logie, Fife, Perthshire
James McLaren	Serv	U	19	Blacksmith	Gargunnock, Stirlingshire
William Robertson	Serv	U	15	Blacksmith apprentice	Gargunnock, Stirlingshire

Meiklewood Rows Lodge

Name	Relation	Status	Age	Occupation	Birthplace
James Barcley	Head	M	35	Railway labourer	Gargunnock, Stirlingshire
Ann Barcley	Wife	M	30	Railway labourer's wife	Campsie, Stirlingshire
William Cowbrough Barclay	Son		9	Scholar	Gargunnock, Stirlingshire
Mary Barclay	Dau		6	Scholar	Gargunnock, Stirlingshire
Catherine Barclay	Dau		4		Gargunnock, Stirlingshire

Name	Relation	Condition	Age	Occupation	Birthplace
Ann Barclay	Dau		I		Gargunnock, Stirlingshire
James Henshilwood	Lodger	U	22	Painter	Lanark, Lanarkshire
Alexander Smith	Lodger	U	18	Painter	Glasgow, Lanarkshire
Patrick Donachy	Lodger	U	17	Painter	Glasgow, Lanarkshire

Woodyett Farmhouse

Name	Relation	Condition	Age	Occupation	Birthplace
John Mailer	Head	M	40	Farmer Of 105 Acres arable Employing 2 men,1 boy, 2 women.	Blackford, Perthshire
Annie Mailer	Wife	M	40	Farmer's wife	St Ninians, Stirlingshire
John Mailer	Son	U	14	Scholar	Gargunnock, Stirlingshire
James Mailer	son		12	Scholar	Gargunnock, Stirlingshire
William Bryce Mailer	Son		11	Scholar	Gargunnock, Stirlingshire
Peter Mailer	Son		9	Scholar	Gargunnock, Stirlingshire
Robert Mailer	Son		8	Scholar	Gargunnock, Stirlingshire
Annie Clark Mailer	Dau		6	Scholar	Gargunnock, Stirlingshire
Margaret Bryce Mailer	Dau		4		Gargunnock, Stirlingshire
Grace Rowan Mailer	Dau		3		Gargunnock, Stirlingshire
David Mailer	Son		3m		Gargunnock, Stirlingshire
Archibald Dewar	Serv	U	22	Farm servant	St Ninians, Stirlingshire
John Dewar	Serv	U	18	Farm servant	St Ninians, Stirlingshire
John Cowbrough	Serv	U	13	Farm servant	Kippen, Stirlingshire
Marion M Gillan	Serv	U	21	Dairymaid (Domestic Servant)	Kilsyth, Stirlingshire
Mary Murray	Serv	U	19	General servant (Domestic)	Arnot, Ayrshire

Meiklewood Porter's Lodge

Name	Relation	Condition	Age	Occupation	Birthplace
William Maxton	Head	M	36	Gardener (Domestic Servant)	Muthill, Perthshire
Margaret Maxton	Wife	M	34	Gardener's wife	Muthill, Perthshire
Ann Maxton	Dau		8	Scholar	Muthill, Perthshire
James Maxton	Son		2		Carmyle, Lanarkshire
Jane McLeish	Sister in Law	U	30	General servant (Domestic)	Muthill, Perthshire

Meiklewood Coachman's House

Name	Relation	Condition	Age	Occupation	Birthplace
Thomas Steward	Head	M	33	Coachman (Domestic Servant)	Mid Calder, Edinburghshire
Ann Stewart	Wife	M	32	Coachman's wife	Aberfeldy, Perthshire
Amilia Jane Stewart	Dau		6		Partick, Glasgow, Lanarkshire
Barbara Stewart	Dau		4		Govan, Renfrewshire
Margaret Stewart	Dau		1		Gargunnock, Stirlingshire
Alexander Cowie	Lodger	W	61	House painter (Grainer)	Old Machar, Aberdeen

Name	Relation	Condition	Age	Occupation	Birthplace
Arnott's House					
John Arnott	Head	U	20	General labourer	Gargunnock, Stirlingshire
Meiklewood House					
Jane Boyes	Head Serv	U	38	Cook (Domestic Servant)	Kirkmaiden, Wigtonshire
Margaret Robertson	Serv	U	32	Laundress (Domestic Servant)	Kinross, Kinross-shire
Mary McGregor	Serv	U	22	Housemaid (Domestic Servant)	Alexandria, Dumbartonshire
Isabella Jeffrey	Serv	U	20	Kitchenmaid (Domestic Servant)	Muiravonside, Stirlingshire
Mains Farmhouse					
Robert Kay	Head	M	41	Farmer of 110 acres arable employing 3 men, 1 boy, 1 girl.	Gargunnock, Stirlingshire
Jane Kay	Wife	M	31	Farmer's wife	Port of Menteith, Perthshire
James Kay	Son		5	Scholar	Gargunnock, Stirlingshire
Mary Christie Kay	Dau		2		Gargunnock, Stirlingshire
John Jaffray	Serv	U	24	Farm servant	St Ninians, Stirlingshire
Gabriel Hunter	Serv	U	18	Farm servant	Cupar, Fife
Alexander Bruce	Serv	U	17	Farm servant	Airth, Stirlingshire
James McIntee	Serv	U	13	Farm servant	St Ninians, Stirlingshire
Mary Strang	Serv	U	19	General servant	Gargunnock, Stirlingshire
Meiklewood Cottage (At old road)					
Robert Stevenson	Head	M	59	Forester	Bannockburn, Stirlingshire
Catherine Stevenson	Wife	M	54	Forester's wife	Ballachulish, Argyllshire
Alexander Stevenson	G/son		2		Gargunnock, Stirlingshire
Lower Redhall Farmhouse					
Robert Mailer	Head	M	27	Farmer of 123 Acres arable employing 3 men and 1 woman.	Kilmadock, Perthshire
Catherine Ross Bessie Mailer	Wife	M	21	Farmer's wife	Kilmadock, Perthshire
John Mailer	Son		1m		Gargunnock, Stirlingshire
William McPherson	Serv	U	20	Farm servant	Hardhill, Linlithgowshire
Peter McGregor	Serv	U	18	Farm servant	Stirling, Stirlingshire
Bridget O'Neil	Serv	U	21	General servant (Domestic)	Raploch, Stirlingshire
John McLaren	Serv	U	16	Farm servant	Gargunnock, Stirlingshire

Upper Redhall Farmhouse

Name	Relation	Cond.	Age	Occupation	Birthplace
Janet Cowbrough	Head	W	55	Farmer of 70 Acres, 10 arable employing 1 boy and 1 girl.	Balfron, Stirlingshire
Henry Cowbrough	Son	U	20	Farmer's son	Gargunnock, Stirlingshire
William Cowbrough	Son	U	17	Farmer's son	Gargunnock, Stirlingshire
Euphemia Monteith	Serv	U	17	Domestic servant	Camelon, Stirlingshire
George McArthur	Serv	U	14	Domestic servant	Edinburgh

Hillhead Farmhouse

Name	Relation	Cond.	Age	Occupation	Birthplace
James Kay	Head	W	93	Farmer of 1200 Acres 13 arable employing 1 man, 1 boy,1 girl.	Gargunnock, Stirlingshire
Thomas Kay	Son	U	50	Farmer's son	Gargunnock, Stirlingshire
Elizabeth Kay	Dau	U	47	Farmer's daughter	Gargunnock, Stirlingshire
Andrew Kay	Son	U	39	Farmer's son	Gargunnock, Stirlingshire
Peter Cowan	Serv	U	17	Farm servant	St Ninians, Stirlingshire
Catherine Menzies	Serv	U	17	Farm servant	Muiravonside, Stirlingshire

Gargunnock Lodge

Name	Relation	Cond.	Age	Occupation	Birthplace
James McLaren	Head	M	61	General labourer	Gargunnock, Stirlingshire
Margaret McLaren	Wife	M	52	Labourer's wife	Killern, Stirlingshire

Gargunnock House

Name	Relation	Cond.	Age	Occupation	Birthplace
John Stirling Stirling	Head	M	40	Colonel (Retd) Royal Artillery and land proprietor.	Barony, Glasgow, Lanarkshire
Henrietta Charlotte Stirling	Wife	M	37	Colonel and land proprietor's wife	St Stephen's, Edinburgh
Louisa Charlotte Stirling	Dau		9	Scholar	England
Charles Stirling	Son		7	Scholar	Killearn, Stirlingshire
Anselan J. B. Stirling	Son		5	Scholar	Barbados
Kathleen C. A Stirling	Dau		4		Ireland
Ann J. Buchanan Kincaid	Sister in Law	U	39	Householder	St Stephen's, Edinburgh.
Anna E Nitschk	Governess	U	20	Governess	Switzerland
Mary Elizabeth Todd	Serv	U	41	Nurse (Domestic Servant)	Barbados
Ellen Barnard	Serv	U	27	Cook (Domestic Servant)	Clackmannan, Clackmannanshire
Mary Meeking	Serv	U	23	Housemaid (Domestic Servant)	Monkton, Ayrshire
Ann Tracy	Serv	U	44	Housemaid (Domestic Servant)	Ireland
Elizabeth McNaught	Serv	U	24	Laundry maid (Domestic Servant)	Tarbolton, Ayrshire
Ellen Arthur	Serv	U	17	Nursery maid (Domestic Servant)	Ayr, Ayrshire
Jane Cowbrough	Serv	U	17	Kitchen maid (Domestic Servant)	Glasgow, Lanarkshire

Gargunnock Coachman's House

Name	Relation	Status	Age	Occupation	Birthplace
Francis Will	Head	M	24	Coachman (Domestic Servant)	Longside, Aberdeen
Williamina Will	Wife	M	25	Coachman's wife	St Cuthbert's, Edinburgh
Andrew Todd	Father in Law	W	56	Former librarian	St Cuthbert's, Edinburgh

Gardener's House

Name	Relation	Status	Age	Occupation	Birthplace
John Elder	Head	M	69	Gardener (Domestic Servant)	Lanark, Lanarkshire
Christian Elder	Wife	M	69	Gardener's wife	Gladsmuir, Haddington

Millthread Cottage

Name	Relation	Status	Age	Occupation	Birthplace
William Bryce	Head	M	57	Distillery manager	Muiravonside, Stirlingshire
Isabella Bryce	Wife	M	56	Distillery manager's wife	Gargunnock, Stirlingshire
Jessie Crystal Bryce	G/dau		6	Scholar	Gargunnock, Stirlingshire
William Crystal Bryce	G/Son		3		Gargunnock, Stirlingshire

Gargunnock Cottage

Name	Relation	Status	Age	Occupation	Birthplace
Margaret McFarlane	Head	U	58	Former dairymaid	Port of Menteith, Perthshire
Catherine Moir	Niece	U	20	General servant	Drymen. Stirlingshire
George Moir	Nephew		14	Scholar	Drymen. Stirlingshire

Owlet Hall (Carpenter's House and Shop)

Name	Relation	Status	Age	Occupation	Birthplace
Peter McLaren	Head	U	60	Master joiner. Employing 5 men and 1 boy.	Gargunnock, Stirlingshire
Robert McLaren	Brother	U	44	Master joiner. Employing 5 men and 1 boy.	Gargunnock, Stirlingshire
Margaret McLaren	Sister	U	66	Retired cook (Domestic Servant)	Gargunnock, Stirlingshire
Janet McLaren	Sister	U	46	General servant (Domestic)	Gargunnock, Stirlingshire
John McLaren	Nephew	U	21	Joiner	England
Andrew Lambert	Serv	U	21	Joiner	Gargunnock, Stirlingshire
William Jamieson	Serv	U	21	Joiner	Gargunnock, Stirlingshire
John Cowbrough	Serv	U	19	Apprentice joiner	Glasgow, Lanarkshire

Fleuchams Farm Barn

Name	Relation	Status	Age	Occupation	Birthplace
John Polleck	Head	W	79	Former farm labourer	Ireland

Schoolhouse

Name	Relation	Status	Age	Occupation	Birthplace
William Jamieson	Head	M	52	Schoolmaster, Inspector of Births Register.	Glasgow, Lanarkshire

Name	Relationship	Condition	Age	Occupation	Birthplace
Janet Jamieson	Wife	M	50	Schoolmaster's wife	Bothwell, Lanarkshire
Jemima Jamieson	Dau		10	Scholar	Gargunnock, Stirlingshire
Jane Jamieson	Dau		8	Scholar	Gargunnock, Stirlingshire
Margaret H Jamieson	Dau		6	Scholar	Gargunnock, Stirlingshire

John Burns's House

Name	Relationship	Condition	Age	Occupation	Birthplace
John Burns	Head	M	53	Retired baker	Denny, Stirlingshire
Margaret Bryson	Sister	W	59	Farmer's widow	Denny, Stirlingshire

Old Malt Barn

Name	Relationship	Condition	Age	Occupation	Birthplace
John Kemp	Head	M	31	Ploughman	Stirling, Stirlingshire
Mary Kemp	Wife	M	33	Ploughman's wife	Bannockburn, Stirlingshire
Elizabeth Kemp	Dau		11	Scholar	St Ninians, Stirlingshire
Isabella Kemp	Dau		9	Scholar	St Ninians, Stirlingshire
Sophia Kemp	Dau		5	Scholar	St Ninians, Stirlingshire
Thomas Kemp	Son		1		St Ninians, Stirlingshire

Old Malt Barn

Name	Relationship	Condition	Age	Occupation	Birthplace
James Wardlaw	Head	W	46	Distillery labourer	Dunfermline, Fife
Adam Wardlaw	Son	U	22	Worsted spinner	Craikry, Clackmannanshire
John Wardlaw	Son	U	20	Lath spinner	Duckhill, Fife
Marion Wardlaw	Dau	U	17	Worsted spinner	Lanemuir, Clackmannanshire
William Wardlaw	Son		3		Alloa, Clackmannanshire

Old Malt Barn

Name	Relationship	Condition	Age	Occupation	Birthplace
William Buchanan	Head	M	32	Agricultural labourer	Bannockburn, Stirlingshire
Christine Buchanan	Wife	M	40	Labourer's wife	Ardrossan, Ayrshire

Rhone Cottage

Name	Relationship	Condition	Age	Occupation	Birthplace
John Cowbrough	Head	M	56	Distillery labourer	Campsie, Stirlingshire
Mary Cowbrough	Wife	M	57	Labourer's wife	Glasgow, Lanarkshire
Archibald Cowbrough	Son		13	Plumber's labourer	Kippen, Stirlingshire
Mary Cowbrough	G/Dau		5		Gargunnock, Stirlingshire

Rhone Cottage

Name	Relationship	Condition	Age	Occupation	Birthplace
William Murdoch	Head	M	63	Master coachbuilder (Retd)	Gargunnock, Stirlingshire
Jane Murdoch	Wife	M	61	Coachbuilder's wife	Newlands, Peebles

Beild of Leckie

Name	Relation	Condition	Age	Occupation	Birthplace
John Lang	Head	M	53	Farmer of 190 Acres arable employing 3 men and 1 boy.	Gargunnock, Stirlingshire
Margaret Lang	Wife	M	40	Farmer's wife	Port of Menteith, Perthshire
Mary Lang	Dau		14	Farmer's daughter	Gargunnock, Stirlingshire
Robert Lang	Son		13	Scholar	Gargunnock, Stirlingshire
Jessie Lang	Dau		11	Scholar	Gargunnock, Stirlingshire
Thomas Lang	Son		9	Scholar	Gargunnock, Stirlingshire
Maggie Lang	Dau		7	Scholar	Gargunnock, Stirlingshire
John Lang	Son		5	Scholar	Gargunnock, Stirlingshire
George Lang	Son		3		Gargunnock, Stirlingshire
James Lang	Son		11m		Gargunnock, Stirlingshire
William Liddle	Servant	U	30	Farm servant	Bannockburn, Stirlingshire
John Dunlop	Servant	U	39	Farm servant	Gargunnock, Stirlingshire
Matthew Miller	Servant	U	18	Farm servant	Stirling, Stirlingshire
John Hutton	Servant	U	15	Farm servant	Kippen, Stirlingshire

Leckie Porter Lodge

Name	Relation	Condition	Age	Occupation	Birthplace
Hugh Mowat	Head	M	52	Gamekeeper	Fettercairn, Kincardineshire
Elizabeth Mowat	Wife	M	48	Gamekeeper's wife	England
Elizabeth Mowat	Dau	U	16	Dressmaker	Kilmelford, Argyllshire

Leckie Old Mansion House

Name	Relation	Condition	Age	Occupation	Birthplace
James Moon	Head	W	65	Overseer Leckie	Comrie, Perthshire
Alexander Moon	Son	U	28	General labourer	Shotts, Lanarkshire
Margery Moon	Dau	U	24	Dressmaker	Gargunnock, Stirlingshire

Leckie Old House

Name	Relation	Condition	Age	Occupation	Birthplace
James Gorham	Head	M	48	General labourer	Tibbermore, Perthshire
Jessie Gorham	Wife	M	48	Labourer's wife	Auchtergaven, Perthshire
Maria Gorham	Dau		15	Labourer's daughter	Tibbermore, Perthshire
William Gorham	Son		13	Scholar	Tibberrmore, Perthshire
Jessie Ann Gorham	Dau		10	Scholar	Tibbermore, Perthshire

Leckie Old House

Name	Relation	Condition	Age	Occupation	Birthplace
John Stalker	Head	U	21	Under gamekeeper	Kincardine, Perthshire

Knock O'Ronald

Name	Relation	Condition	Age	Occupation	Birthplace
Robert Downie	Head	W	57	Farmer of 800 Acres 80 acres arable	Kilmadock, Perthshire

Name	Relation	Condition	Age	Occupation	Birthplace
William Downie	Son	U	33	Farmer's son	Stirling, Stirlingshire
Elizabeth H. Downie	Dau	U	31	Farmer's daughter	Stirling, Stirlingshire
Mary Downie	Dau	U	29	Farmer's daughter	Stirling, Stirlingshire
Robert Downie	Son	U	17	Farmer's son	Stirling, Stirlingshire
Robert McLeod	Serv	U	21	Farm servant	Stirling, Stirlingshire

Spittalton

Name	Relation	Condition	Age	Occupation	Birthplace
John McEwan	Head	W	86	Farmer 300 Acres 125 arable employing 4 men 1 girl 1 boy	Drymen, Stirlingshire
Thomas McEwan	Son	U	56	Farmer's son	Drymen, Stirlingshire
Alexander McEwan	Son	U	54	Farmer's son	Drymen, Stirlingshire
Andrew McEwan	Son	U	52	Farmer's son	Drymen, Stirlingshire
Marjory McEwan	Dau	U	58	Farmer's daughter	Drymen, Stirlingshire
Thomas McEwan	Nephew	U	28	Farmer's servant	Drymen, Stirlingshire
Helen Kerrigen	Serv	U	21	Farm servant (Domestic)	Gargunnock, Stirlingshire
George Forsyth	Serv	U	14	Farm servant (Domestic)	Buchanan, Stirlingshire

Crawtree

Name	Relation	Condition	Age	Occupation	Birthplace
Thomas McFarlane	Head	M	53	Farmer of 149 Acres arable employing 3 men	Cumbernauld, Dumbartonshire
Agnes G. McFarlane	Wife	M	67	Farmer's wife	Muiravonside, Stirlingshire
Robert McFarlane	Son	U	26	Farmer's son	Slamannan, Stirlingshire
Agnes McFarlane	Dau	U	24	Farmer's daughter	Slamannan, Stirlingshire
Jane McFarlane	Dau	U	22	Farmer's daughter	Slamannan, Stirlingshire
Andrew Liddel	Serv	U	20	Farmer's servant	Linlithgow, Linlithgowshire
Allan Smith	Serv	U	16	Farmer's servant	Cumbernauld, Dumbartonshire
William Smith	Serv	U	15	Farmer's servant	Linlithgow, Linlithgowshire

Birkenwood

Name	Relation	Condition	Age	Occupation	Birthplace
James Gray	Head	M	44	Farmer of 115 Acres arable employing 2 men, 1 boy, 1 girl	St Ninians, Stirlingshire
Elizabeth Gray	Wife	M	42	Farmer's wife	St Ninians, Stirlingshire
James Gary	Son	U	19	Farmer's son	Gargunnock, Stirlingshire
Henry Gray	Son	U	17	Farmer's son	Gargunnock, Stirlingshire
Thomas Gray	Son		15	Grain merchant	Gargunnock, Stirlingshire
Agnes Gray	Dau		13	Scholar	Gargunnock, Stirlingshire
John Gray	Son		10	Scholar	Gargunnock, Stirlingshire
Elizabeth Gray	Dau		8	Scholar	Gargunnock, Stirlingshire

Name	Relation	Cond.	Age	Occupation	Birthplace
Andrew Gray	Son		7	Scholar	Gargunnock, Stirlingshire
Sarah Hendry	Serv		14	General domestic servant	Slamannan, Stirlingshire
Robert Spiers	Serv		15	Farm servant	Muiravonside,Stirlingshire
Mosshead					
Edward Moir	Head	M	41	Farm labourer	Balquhidder, Perthshire
Mary Moir	Wife	M		Farm labourer's wife	
Inch Of Leckie					
Samuel F. Bain	Head	M	44	Farmer 122 Acres arable employing 1 man	Gargunnock, Stirlingshire
Grace W. Bain	Wife	M	38	Farmer's wife	Culross, Clackmannanshire
William Bain	Son	U	18	Farmer's son	Gargunnock, Stirlingshire
Christina Bain	Dau	U	15	Farmer's daughter	Gargunnock, Stirlingshire
John H. Bain	Son		13	Farmer's son	Gargunnock, Stirlingshire
Janet F. Bain	Dau		11	Scholar	Gargunnock, Stirlingshire
Samuel Bain	Son		9	Scholar	Gargunnock, Stirlingshire
Mary Bain	Dau		6		Gargunnock, Stirlingshire
James Bain	Son		4		Gargunnock, Stirlingshire
Alexander Bain	Son		1		Gargunnock, Stirlingshire
Peter Wilson	Serv	U	16	Farm servant	Polmont, Stirlingshire
Culmore Railway Cottage					
John Arnot	Head	M	43	Railway labourer	Bathgate, Linlithgow.
Jane Arnot	Wife	M	44	Labourer's wife	Gargunnock, Stirlingshire
William Arnot	Son	U	18	General labourer	Alloa, Clackmannanshire
James Arnot	Son		11	Scholar	Gargunnock, Stirlingshire
Archibald Arnot	Son		11	Scholar	Gargunnock, Stirlingshire
Robert Arnot	Son		8	Scholar	Gargunnock, Stirlingshire
Charles Arnot	Son		6	Scholar	Gargunnock, Stirlingshire
Hugh Arnot	Son		4		Gargunnock, Stirlingshire
Henry Arnot	Son		1		Gargunnock, Stirlingshire
Isabella Arnot	Dau		13	Scholar	Gargunnock, Stirlingshire
West Culmore					
Margaret Risk	Head	W	46	Farmer of 100 Acres arable	Kippen, Stirlingshire
William Risk	Son	U	24	Farmer's son	Drymen, Stirlingshire
Jane Risk	Dau	U	18	Farmer's daughter	Drymen, Stirlingshire
James Risk	Son	U	16	Farmer's son	Kippen, Stirlingshire

Name	Relation	Status	Age	Occupation	Birthplace
Eliza Risk	Dau	U	15	Farmer's daughter	Gargunnock, Stirlingshire
George Jack	Serv	U	16	Farm servant	Stirling, Stirlingshire

East Culmore

Name	Relation	Status	Age	Occupation	Birthplace
Alexander McGregor	Head	M	41	Farmer of 114 Acres arable employing 2 men,1 boy,1 girl.	Gargunnock, Stirlingshire
Elizabeth McGregor	Wife	M	37	Farmer's wife	Gargunnock, Stirlingshire
Charles McGregor	Son		8	Scholar	Gargunnock, Stirlingshire
James McGregor	Son		7	Scholar	Gargunnock, Stirlingshire
Jane M McGregor	Dau		5	Scholar	Gargunnock, Stirlingshire
Isabella McGregor	Dau		4		Gargunnock, Stirlingshire
Elizabeth McGregor	Dau		2		Gargunnock, Stirlingshire
Alexander McGregor	Dau		5m		Gargunnock, Stirlingshire
James Menzie	Serv	U	55	Farm servant	Perth, Perthshire
Robert McGregor	Serv	U	17	Farm servant	Cleish, Kinross
James Pirrie	Serv	U	16	Farm servant	Dunfermline, Fife
Jane Thomson	Serv	U	23	Domestic servant	Falkirk, Stirlingshire

Culbeg

Name	Relation	Status	Age	Occupation	Birthplace
John Fisher	Head	U	32	In charge for the Trustees of a farm of 80 Acres arable employing 3 men, 2 girls.	Gargunnock, Stirlingshire
Janet Fisher	Sister	U	27	Residenter	Gargunnock, Stirlingshire
Elizabeth Fisher	Sister	U	25	Residenter	Gargunnock, Stirlingshire
Christina Bain	Visitor	W	78	Sick nurse	Alloa, Clackmannanshire.
William Smith	Serv	U	39	Farm servant	Muiravonside, Stirlingshire
Duncan Thompson	Serv	U	17	Farm servant	Gartmore, Perthshire
Moses Taylor	Serv	U	26	Farm servant	Gargunnock, Stirlingshire
Catherine McLachlan	Serv	U	16	Domestic servant	Dumblane, Perthshire

Leckieburn Railway Cottage

Name	Relation	Status	Age	Occupation	Birthplace
Peter McLaren	Head	M	36	Railway labourer	Auchterarder, Perthshire
Margaret McLaren	Wife	M	26	Labourer's wife	Ireland
Mary McLaren	Dau		10	Scholar	Glasgow, Lanarkshire
Robert McLaren	Son		8	Scholar	Kippen, Stirlingshire
Peter McLaren	Son		2		Kippen, Stirlingshire
Hannah McLaren	Dau		8m		Kippen, Stirlingshire

Greenfoot

Name	Relation	Status	Age	Occupation	Birthplace
James Sands	Head	U	33	Farmer of 125 Acres arable employing 3 men !boy and 1 woman.	Gargunnock, Stirlingshire
Mary Sands	Mother	W	70	Farmer's mother	Gargunnock, Stirlingshire
Agnes Sands	Sister	U	29	Farmer's Sister	Gargunnock, Stirlingshire
Alexander Mitchell	Serv	U	23	Farm Servant	Drymen, Stirlingshire
Robert Fawcett	Serv	U	20	Farm Servant	Kippen, Stirlingshire
Alexander Graham	Serv	U	16	Farm servant	Kippen, Stirlingshire
James Aitken	Serv	U	15	Farm servant	St Ninians, Stirlingshire
Isabella Waugh	Serv	U	19	Dairymaid	Larbert, Stirlingshire

Nether Carse Railway Cottage

Name	Relation	Status	Age	Occupation	Birthplace
Robert Lambert	Head	M	47	Railway labourer	Dunblane, Perthshire
Eliza Lambert	Wife	M	46	Labourer's wife	Gargunnock, Stirlingshire
John Lambert	Son		11	Scholar	Gargunnock, Stirlingshire
Mary Lambert	Dau		14		Gargunnock, Stirlingshire

Nether Carse

Name	Relation	Status	Age	Occupation	Birthplace
Alexander Moir	Head	M	30	Farmer of 123 acres arable employing 2 men, 2 girls, 1 boy.	Kincardine, Perthshire
Elizabeth Moir	Wife	M	28	Farmer's wife	Kippen, Stirlingshire
James Moir	Son		4		Gargunnock, Stirlingshire
Alexander Moir	Son		2		Gargunnock, Stirlingshire
John Moir	Son		7m		Gargunnock, Stirlingshire
Peter Jack	Serv	U	26	Farm servant	Kincardine, Perthshire
John Bruce	Serv	U	19	Farm servant	St Ninians, Stirlingshire
Andrew Meiklejohn	Serv	U	16	Farm servant	Saline, Fife
Mary Hannah	Serv	U	22	General servant (Domestic)	Falkirk, Stirlingshire
Jean Malcolm	Serv	U	14	General servant (Domestic)	West Kilbride, Lanarkshire

Patrickston

Name	Relation	Status	Age	Occupation	Birthplace
James McKenzie	Head	M	45	Farm servant	Port of Monteith, Perthshire
Janet McKenzie	Wife	M	43	Farm servant's wife	Kippen, Stirlingshire
Mary McKenzie	Dau		12	Scholar	Kincardine, Perthshire
James McKenzie	Son		5		Kincardine, Perthshire

Kepdarroch

Name	Relation	Status	Age	Occupation	Birthplace
John Inglis	Head	M	65	Farmer of 250 Acres arable employing 2 men and 1 girl.	St Ninians, Stirlingshire

Name	Relationship	Condition	Age	Occupation	Birthplace
Margaret Inglis	Wife	M	55	Farmer's wife	Gargunnock, Stirlingshire
William Lang Inglis	Son	U	22	Farmer's son	Gargunnock, Stirlingshire
Robert Inglis	Son	U	21	Farmer's son	Gargunnock, Stirlingshire
Alexander Inglis	Son	U	20	Farmer's son	Gargunnock, Stirlingshire
Ann McNaughton Inglis	Dau	U	17	Farmer's daughter	Gargunnock, Stirlingshire
Margaret Inglis	Dau	U	15	Farmer's daughter	Gargunnock, Stirlingshire
John Inglis	Son		13	Scholar	Gargunnock, Stirlingshire
William Hutton	Serv	M	38	Farm servant	Airth, Stirlingshire
John Marshall	Serv	U	18	Farm servant	Cumbernauld, Dumbartonshire
Mary Quean	Serv	U	17	Domestic servant	Cumbernauld, Dumbartonshire

Kepdarroch Railway Cottage

Name	Relationship	Condition	Age	Occupation	Birthplace
Janet McBeth	Head	W	50	Railway labourer's mother	Alloa, Clackmannanshire
Charles McBeth	Son	U	21	Railway labourer	Drymen, Stirlingshire
William McBeth	Son		13		Drymen, Stirlingshire
Robina McBeth	Dau		10	Scholar	Drymen, Stirlingshire

Piperland

Name	Relationship	Condition	Age	Occupation	Birthplace
James Robertson	Head	M	50	Railway labourer	Lanark, Lanarkshire
Isabella Robertson	Wife	M	40	Labourer's wife	Eckford, Roxburghshire
John Robertson	Son	U	19	Railway fireman	Gargunnock, Stirlingshire
Agnes Robertson	Dau	U	17	Labourer's daughter	Gargunnock, Stirlingshire
George Robertson	Son		12	Scholar	Gargunnock, Stirlingshire
Robert Robertson	Son		11	Scholar	Gargunnock, Stirlingshire
Alexander Robertson	Son		5		Gargunnock, Stirlingshire
Hall Robertson	Son		4		Gargunnock, Stirlingshire
Charles Robertson	Son		2		Gargunnock, Stirlingshire

Burnton

Name	Relationship	Condition	Age	Occupation	Birthplace
Alexander McGlashan	Head	M	79	Agricultural labourer	Gargunnock, Stirlingshire
Margaret McGlashan	Dau	U	40	Labourer's daughter	Gargunnock, Stirlingshire

Burnton

Name	Relationship	Condition	Age	Occupation	Birthplace
John McCallum	Head	M	65	Wright employing 1 man, 2 boys, 1girl.	Gargunnock, Stirlingshire
Helen McCallum	Wife	M	51	Wright's wife	Buchlyvie, Stirlingshire
Janet McCallum	Dau		12	Scholar	Gargunnock, Stirlingshire
John McCallum	Son		8	Scholar	Gargunnock, Stirlingshire
James Harvey	Boarder	U	31	Wright and joiner	Kippen, Stirlingshire

Name	Relationship	Status	Age	Occupation	Place of Birth
Robert Moon	Boarder	U	17	Apprentice wright	Gargunnock, Stirlingshire
Edward Watson	Boarder	U	18	Apprentice wright	Kippen, Stirlingshire
Janet McLeallan	Serv	U	14	Domestic servant	Slamannan, Stirlingshire
Burnton					
Margaret Evetts	Wife (Head)	M	28	Butler's wife	Kippen, Stirlingshire
Margaret Patterson Evetts	Dau		1		Fintry, Stirlingshire
Margaret Findley	Mother in Law	W	52	Butler's Mother in Law	Glasgow, Lanarkshire
Burnton					
John Neilson	Head	M	28	Farm servant	Cumbernauld, Dumbartonshire
Christina Neilson	Wife	M	27	Farm servant's wife	Old Monkland, Lanarkshire
Agnes Neilson	Dau		6		Barony, Glasgow, Lanarkshire
Christina Neilson	Dau		4		Gargunnock, Stirlingshire
Isabella Neilson	Dau		2		Gargunnock, Stirlingshire
James Neilson	Brother	U	22	Mason	Chryston, Lanarkshire
Burnton					
James Wingate	Head	U	57	Master blacksmith	Gargunnock, Stirlingshire
Christina Wingate	Sister	U	53	Master blacksmith's sister	Gargunnock, Stirlingshire
Robert Kerr	Serv	U	26	Blacksmith (J/Man)	Falkirk, Stirlingshire
Peter McLaren	Serv	U	18	Apprentice blacksmith	Lecropt, Perthshire
Burnton					
John Hamilton	Head	M	35	Ploughman	Kippen, Stirlingshire
Agnes Hamilton	Wife	M	34	Ploughman's wife	New Monkland, Lanarkshire
Samuel Hamilton	Son		12	Ploughman's son	Kippen, Stirlingshire
Sarah Hamilton	Dau		9	Scholar	Kippen, Stirlingshire
Agnes Hamilton	Dau		6	Scholar	Kippen, Stirlingshire
Alexander Hamilton	Son	3	3		Gargunnock, Stirlingshire
John Hamilton	Son				Gargunnock, Stirlingshire
James Hamilton	Son		1		Gargunnock, Stirlingshire
Myreton Farm					
John S Waddell	Head	M	56	Farmer of 200 Acres	Kilpatrick, Dumbartonshire
Jane Waddell	Wife	M	50	Farmer's wife	Kilmaronack, Dumbartonshire
George Waddell	Son	U	19	Farmer's son	Gargunnock, Stirlingshire
Martha Waddell	Dau	U	18	Farmer's daughter	Gargunnock, Stirlingshire
Grace Waddell	Dau	U	17	Farmer's daughter	Gargunnock, Stirlingshire

Name	Relation	Condition	Age	Occupation	Birthplace
Wm Buchannan Waddell	Son		14	Farmer's son	Gargunnock, Stirlingshire
Agnes Waddell	Dau		11	Scholar	Gargunnock, Stirlingshire
John Smellie Waddell	Son		10	Scholar	Gargunnock, Stirlingshire

Fourmerks Farm

Name	Relation	Condition	Age	Occupation	Birthplace
William Johnston	Head	M	68	Farmer of 100 Acres arable employing 1 man, 1 woman,1 boy.	St Ninians, Stirlingshire
Margaret Johnston	Wife	M	60	Farmer's wife	Kippen, Stirlingshire
Robert Makison	Serv	U	28	Farm Servant	Kippen, Stirlingshire
Helen Jack	Serv	U	24	Farm Servant	Muthill, Perthshire
James Leckie	Serv	U	16	farm Servant	Kippen, Stirlingshire

Old Hall

Name	Relation	Condition	Age	Occupation	Birthplace
James Mackison	Head	M	75	Farmer of 80 Acres arable	Gargunnock, Stirlingshire
Agnes Mackison	Wife	M	60	Farmer's wife	Gargunnock, Stirlingshire
Mary Mackison	Dau	U	32	Farmer's daughter	Kippen, Stirlingshire
Eliza Mackison	Dau	U	27	Farmer's daughter	Kippen, Stirlingshire
Charles Mackison	Son	U	25	Farmer's son	Kippen, Stirlingshire
James Mackison	Son	U	23	Farmer's son	Kippen, Stirlingshire
Agnes Mackison	Dau	U	20	Farmer's daughter	Kippen, Stirlingshire

Ballochleam

Name	Relation	Condition	Age	Occupation	Birthplace
William McFarlane	Head	M	60	Farmer employing 1 man, 1 boy	Port of Menteith, Perthshire
Barbara McFarlane	Wife	M	32	Farmer's wife	Bankfoot, Perthshire
Jessie McFarlane	Dau		12	Scholar	Gargunnock, Stirlingshire
George McFarlane	Son		7	Scholar	Gargunnock, Stirlingshire
Maggie McFarlane	Dau		5		Gargunnock, Stirlingshire
David McFarlane	Son		2		Gargunnock, Stirlingshire
Helen Kennedy	Serv	U	21	General servant (Domestic)	Gargunnock, Stirlingshire
James Maxwell	Serv	U	17	Farm servant	St Ninians, Stirlingshire
John Huggart	Serv		14	Farm servant	Ardoch, Perthshire

Burnfoot

Name	Relation	Condition	Age	Occupation	Birthplace
Archibald McDermid	Head	U	30	Farmer of 1000 acres 40 arable	Garsmorchy, Argyllshire
Peter McDermid	Brother	U	28	Farmer's brother	Garsmorchy, Argyllshire
Malcolm McColl	Serv	U	26	Farm servant and shepherd	Garsmorchy, Argyllshire
Janet Docharty	Serv	U	28	Farm servant	Old Monkland, Lanarkshire

Boquhan Mansion House

Name	Relationship	M/U	Age	Occupation	Birthplace
George Best McNair	Head	M	45	Coalmaster	Shettleston, Lanarkshire
Frances Dorothy McNair	Wife	M	47	Coalmaster's wife	England
Frances Elianor McNair	Dau	U	18	Scholar	Glasgow, Lanarkshire
Emily Edith McNair	Dau		15	Scholar	Glasgow, Lanarkshire
Mary Christian McNair	Dau		12	Scholar	Glasgow, Lanarkshire
James Herbert McNair	Son		10	Scholar	Glasgow, Lanarkshire
Mildred Helen McNair	Dau		8	Scholar	Glasgow, Lanarkshire
Philip Lionel Hope McNair	Son		5		Largs, Ayrshire
Caroline Gertrude McNair	Dau				Largs, Ayrshire
James Stimcer McNair	Brother	U	57	Retd Military Officer	New Brunswick
Bertha Elise Palmie	Serv	U	31	Governess	Poysia, Germany
Mary Monro	Serv	U	40	Cook (Domestic Servant)	Kilbrundon, Argyllshire
Margaret Douglas	Serv	U	26	Nurse (Domestic Servant)	Elgin, Morayshire
Agnes Wright Armstrong	Serv	U	27	Table maid (Domestic Servant)	Port of Menteith, Perthshire
Ann Hossack	Serv	U	37	Laundry Maid (Domestic Servant)	Inverness, Inverness-shire
Mary Crawford	Serv	U	21	Housemaid (Domestic Servant)	Stirling, Stirlingshire
Jack A Toboulor	Serv	U	23	Coachman (Domestic Servant)	Greenock, Renfrewshire

Boquhan Gardener's Lodge

Name	Relationship	M/U	Age	Occupation	Birthplace
John Hall	Head	M	55	Gardener	Jedburgh, Roxbough
Elizabeth Hall	Wife	M	55	Gardener's wife	Sorn, Ayrshire
Jessie Hall	Dau	U	19	Gardener's daughter	Gargunnock, Stirling
Mark Robertson	Boarder		14	Gardener's apprentice	Gargunnock, Stirling

Boquhan Farmhouse

Name	Relationship	M/U	Age	Occupation	Birthplace
William Matson	Head	M	58	Estate overseer	St Ninians, Stirlingshire
Margaret Matson	Wife	M	64	Overseer's wife	Gargunnock, Stirling
Peter Matson	Son	U	25	Farm servant	Gargunnock, Stirling
William Matson	Son	U	22	Farm servant	Gargunnock, Stirling
Maggie Matson	G/Dau		15	Scholar	Gargunnock, Stirling.
Mary McDougall	Serv	U	18	Dairymaid	Kilmaronock, Dumbartonshire.

Railway Lodge (Fordhead)

Name	Relationship	M/U	Age	Occupation	Birthplace
Joseph Hamilton	Head	M	55	Railway labourer	Ireland.
Jean Hamilton	Wife	M	49	Labourer's wife	Kippen, Stirlingshire
Catherine Hamilton	Dau		12	Scholar	Kippen, Stirlingshire
Elizabeth Hamilton	Dau		10	Scholar	Kippen, Stirlingshire
Samuel Hamilton	G/Son		1		Gargunnock, Stirlingshire

Fordhead

Name	Relation		Age	Occupation	Birthplace
John More	Head	M	46	Farmer of 110 Acres Employing 2 men , 2 women.	Kippen, Stirlingshire
Isabella More	Wife	M	30	Farmer's wife	Drymen, Stirlingshire.
William More	Son		6	Scholar	Gargunnock, Stirlingshire
Isabella More	Dau		5		Gargunnock, Stirlingshire
James More	Son		3		Gargunnock, Stirlingshire
John More	Son		1		Gargunnock, Stirlingshire
David More	Son		1m		Gargunnock, Stirlingshire
Henry Peddie	Serv		31	Farm servant	Bothkennar, Stirlingshire
John Stewart	G/Son	U	25	Farmer's grandson	Gargunnock, Stirlingshire
Archibald P Stewart	G/Son	U	24	Farmer's grandson	Gargunnock, Stirlingshire
Margaret L Stewart	G/Dau	U	22	Farmer's grand-daughter	Gargunnock, Stirlingshire
Janet Stewart	G/Dau	U	20	Farmer's grand-daughter	Gargunnock, Stirlingshire
Eliza Stewart	G/Dau	U	18	Farmer's grand-daughter	Gargunnock, Stirlingshire

Boquhan Porter's Lodge

Name	Relation		Age	Occupation	Birthplace
Jane Kerr	Head	U	60	Dressmaker	Kippen, Stirlingshire
Catherine Johnston	Niece	U	27	Dressmaker	Glasgow, Lanarkshire

GLOSSARY

A

acting rank	temporary rank, often given for a probationary period prior to substantive rank being awarded
advocate	Scottish solicitor, a member of the Society of Advocates
ag lab	agricultural labourer
alienate	to sell property
app.	apprentice
apparent heir	the future heir who has yet to complete his title
appraiser	the person appointed to value goods.
Argyllshire Highlanders	regiment raised in 1794 as the 98th of Foot then the 91st, linked in 1881 with the Sutherland Highlanders to form the 1st Battalion Argyll and Sutherland Highlanders (Princess Louise's)
arrest	property or cash seized under legal authority.
assembly	meeting of a congregation or Kirk Session. General assembly of the Church of Scotland
Asiatic cholera	true cholera as opposed to similar cholera type diseases
assidation	the act of letting or assigning a lease
assig.	assignation
assize	trial by jury
assup.	assumption, adoption
astrict	tie lands to a mill, where all the grain must be ground; to legally bind
aumbry	cupboard made of wood
avail	to value

B

bailliary	the area under the jurisdiction of a baillie
baillie	officer in a barony; an official of a burgh next in rank to the provost one acting for the person granting a sasine
bannock	a round flat cake, usually of oat-, barley- or pease meal, baked on a girdle
baron	the lowest rank of nobility
barony	lands held by a baron who held them from the Crown with certain rights of jurisdiction. A court held by a baron or his deputy.
battalion	In 1914 the British army consisted of 157 infantry battalions. A WW1 infantry battalion was normally between 900 and 1000 strong. Generally commanded by a Lt Colonel, the unit consisted of one headquarters company and four rifle companies
baulk	ridge or strip of uncultivated ground lying between two portions of ploughed land
bawbee	Scots coin, originally valued at 6 Scots pennies (see currency)
baxter	baker
bear, bere, bigg	barley, hardier and coarser being four or six rows, as opposed to the ordinary two row type
bigging	building, cottage
billeting party	a small party, normally of administrative type soldiers who move ahead of the main body of troops arranging accommodation for the unit
birlawman	normally a senior, respected person appointed to make judgements and act as a juror in the barony or birlaw court
Bodle	Scots coin (see currency)
boll	dry weight, usually a measure of grain (see weights and measures)
bond	an agreement in writing, legally binding the person to repay money
bonnet laird	small landowner who farmed his own land
Books of Adjournal	records of the Justiciary court.
Books of Council and Session	register of deeds in the Court of Session.
bounty	gratuity added to a servant's pay
bothy	separate building on a farm used as accommodation for unmarried labourers: rough hut on the hill used by shepherds
box-bed	bed enclosed in wooden panelling, having either sliding doors, hinged doors, or curtains
brigade	a WW1 infantry brigade consisted of four infantry battalions, a fighting strength of about 3200 men. Normally commanded by a brigadier

brose	oatmeal to which hot water has been added

C

c.	circa (about); c. 1700 = about 1700
Camerons	highland clan whose lands were at the south western end of the Great Glen, Lochaber. Fiercely loyal to the Stewart cause the clan was at the forefront of the 1745 rebellion
Candlemas	Scottish quarter day, 2nd February
capon	fowl
car	sledge
carle	common man, labourer (Carlstoun, town of the carles)
carriage	transporting goods over distance, normally on behalf of the feudal superior as part of a feu agreement
Cateran	Highland marauder
cautioner	one acting as a surety, guarantor
cayne, cain	rent paid in kind
cen.	census
chalder	dry weight, usually lime, malt or grain. (see weights and measures)
chamber-ley	urine
charter	deed granted usually by the feudal superior
Chelsea P.	Chelsea pensioner (sometimes Chelsea out pensioner) single soldier over 65
chopin	liquid measure (see weights and measures)
cite	summon to appear in court
clachan	small settlement
clare constat	document recognising the right to inherit and be infeft, meaning it clearly appears
clarty, clatty	dirty, filthy
cholera	often fatal infectious disease caused by faeces contaminated water and food. Symptom are profuse diarrhoea, vomiting and cramps
chronic	any long standing illness
Commissariat Court	dealt mainly with confirmation of testaments, the appointment of executors and small debts
commissary	judge presiding over Commissary court
commissioners of supply	appointed to collect land tax and oversee matters relating to roads
commonty	common pasture land, used or possessed in common
company	a component part of an infantry battalion; four fighting companies and a headquarter company normally make up a battalion. Fighting companies could be 120 - 160 men strong, usually commanded by a major. Headquarter company strength approx 250 men mainly administrative personnel, again commanded by a major. The company is further sub divided into three or four platoons each with a headquarter element
Company Quartermaster Sergeant (CQMS)	member of the Quartermaster's (QM) department attached to individual companies as the QM's representative and acts as a liaison between the company and the QM. Normally of Colour Sergeant rank. He is responsible for keeping the company supplied with all materials including food and water but not generally ammunition
Company Sergeant Major (Warrant Officer 2	the senior non commissioned officer in the company. Major responsibilities are discipline, organisation of company headquarters, ammo resupply, prisoners of war and training within the company
compear	appear in person, usually in an legal action
cordiner / cordwainer	shoemaker
lance corporal / corporal	two junior non commissioned officer ranks (JNCO). The corporal commands and is responsible for a section of men normally between ten and twelve strong. The lance corporal assists with the administration and commands a half section if required
corps	broadly the army services, as opposed to fighting regiments, though the cavalry regiments en-mass are called the Armoured Corps. Generally, corps are service units like ordnance, medical, pioneer, and catering corps
cottar	tenant occupying a small cottage and perhaps holding a small piece of land usually in return for his labour
couple	pair of rafters forming a V shape roof support

covenanter	supporter of the National Covenant signed in 1638
craig	rock, cliff face; lime craig
crock	old ewe
croft	small piece of enclosed land. small holding.
crofter	a person who occupies a small holding

D

D. or dau or daur	daughter
darg	day's work
dative	executor or tutor appointed by a court
deacon	layman or woman of the Presbyterian Church elected to manage the temporal affairs of a congregation
deed	formal document, signed and witnessed
defender	person against whom a court action is brought
delfs	clods, sods
desposition	evidence on oath.
dispone	convey land, make over, grant
disposition	deed by which property is transferred to another person.
Disruption	split in the Established Church of Scotland, forming the Free Church in 1843
dissenter	non conformist
ditto, do	a repeat of what has already been written
divot	sod, thin slice of turf; peat
dom.	domicile
dom. servt.	domestic servant
domicile	permanent residence
dyke	mound of earth or wall of stones

E

earl	rank of nobility immediately under a marquess and above a vis count
Elder	Presbyterian Church official, elected and ordained to partake in church government as a member of the Kirk Session.
ell	standard length, usually of cloth (see weights and measures)
entail	settlement of succession to heritable property
extent	valuation of land (of old extent)

F

fall	linear measurement (see weights and measurements)
farmtoun	agricultural settlement
fash	trouble, annoy, anger, trouble oneself,
ferme	annual payment of rent, frequently in kind
feu	feudal tenure of land
feu ferme	rent due under the feu charter.
feu maill	rent paid for the feu to the superior
feuar	person who holds the fee to a property
firlot	dry measure (see weights and measures)
flesher	butcher
fornicator	man found guilty of fornication
fornicatrix	woman found guilty of fornication
freeman	person having the freedom of a burgh; a burgess

G

gallon	liquid measurement (see weights and measures)
gear	moveable goods, possessions
General Assembly	highest court in the Church of Scotland or the Free Church
Gen. Disp and Settl.	general disposition and settlement (a will)
gill	liquid measure (see weights and measures)
glebe	land allocated to a minister of a parish in addition to his stipend
grassum	single payment made on entry to a lease or feu, paid again at renewal
groat	Scots coin
gruel	porridge, food made with oatmeal
guidwife	mistress of a farm
guildry	incorporation of merchants in a burgh

H

haill	whole
heritor	proprietor of heritable property; landowner liable for payment of public burdens connected with the parish, schools, poor fund and church property
Highland Light Infantry	regiment raised in 1787 in Argyll, amalgamated in 1959 with the Royal Scots Fusiliers to form 'The Royal Highland Fusiliers' (Princess Margaret's Own Glasgow and Ayrshire Regiment)
horn, put to the	proclaimed an outlaw or bankrupt
host	large armed body of men; the Highland host, 5000 Highlanders assembled by the government in 1678 in an attempt to cow the covenanters of Ayrshire and the south west.

I

ilk	the same thing or person, of that ilk, the same name; usually given to the chief of a clan.
infantry	traditionally soldiers who march into battle and fight on foot. In combat their aim is to close with and kill the enemy
infeft	act of putting a person in heritable possession of land
infield	one of the two main divisions of a farm before crop rotation; best land, nearest the farmhouse, kept in constant cultivation, receiving most of the available manure

J

jougs	instrument of public humiliation consisting of an iron collar and length of chain, normally fixed to a wall or pillar. The collar was locked around the neck of the offender

K

kail	type of cabbage
kain/cain	payment from tenants, usually in kind
kain fowl	fowl payable by tenant to the landlord, at Christmas time
kindly tenant	occupying land at the good will of the owner but having a kind of traditional hereditary right to do so
kindness	claim to customary inheritance through kinship with the previous occupier
King's Own Scottish Borderers.	regiment raised in Edinburgh in 1689, recruiting area is mainly south of Edinburgh and the borders of Scotland: now part of the Scottish Lowland Division
Kirk	Church of Scotland
kirklands	lands of which the church was the superior
Kirn	the last sheaf or handful of corn of the harvest
kist	large box or chest

L

lab	labourer
lade	channel bringing water to a mill, mill stream
lady day	term day (25 March); when contracts were made and terminated
lair	burial plot, grave
laird	owner of landed property, a small estate, Highland chief
Lammas	Scottish quarter day, 1st August
lang	long
liferent	possession of property for the duration of a lifetie, without the right to dispose of the property
lime quarry	stone, quick lime used as mortar, cement. Lime craig, a limestone
lint	flax
lippie	dry measure (see weight and measures)
Loos, Battle of	a co-ordinated assault by the British at Loos and the French at Vimy Ridge between 25th September and 14th October 1915. The British sustained about 60,000 casualties. The engagement cost Sir John French his position as British Commander in Chief
lug	protruding part; a person's or animal's ear
lum	chimney, smoke vent

M

mail, maill	rent
mailing	land on which rent is due
manse	parish minister's residence
march	boundary or frontier
marquess	title or rank of nobility. Between that of a duke and an earl
Mar's year	name given to the rebellion of 1715, when the Jacobite army was led by the Earl of Mar
mart	carcass of beasts killed at Martinmas: animal due as rent to be paid at Martinmas
Martinmas	Scottish quarter day, 11 November
mason	tradesman working in stone
meal	specifically oatmeal as distinct from other kinds, which have defining terms
merk	Scots coin worth 13s.4d. Scots (see currency)
merkland	old Scots measure of land
Michaelmas	29 September. harvest moon, a time for Highland and border raids
midden	dunghill, compost heap, domestic ash-pit, refuse collection point
minor	young person between 12-21 (female) or 14-21 (male). Generally taken to be anyone under the age of 21
mortcloth	black satin or velvet cloth used to cover the coffin en route to the grave, rented from Kirk Session with profits going to the Parish Poor Fund
multure	grain taken by the miller or owner of the mill for grinding corn

N

notar, notery	person licensed to record legal transactions : notary public a clerk of the court
novodamus	formal renewal of a grant by a feudal superior, in order to alter or correct a former grant

O

outfarm	outlying farm worked by a manager or tenant
outfield	poorer less fertile ground, away from the farm steadings
oxgate / oxgang	old Scots measure of land based on the area which an ox could plough in a day; usually one eighth of a ploughgate

P

P.	pensioner (usually Army or Navy)
packman	peddler: travelling merchant
park	enclosed piece of farm land
parish	church administrative area
particate	measurement of land (see weights and measures)
Passchendaele (3rd Battle of Ypres)	Gen Haig's much debated and criticised plan called for an attack in Flanders Jul-Nov 1917. The already waterlogged terrain was reduced to a sea of mud by incessant rain. It was then churned into a quagmire by an artillery barrage which lasted two weeks and fired over 4 million shells. The offensive cost over 250,000 casualties, 90,000 of whom were reported missing. 40,000 were never found having sunk into the mud; 80 years later French farmers still plough up their bones
pasturage	right to graze one's cattle on anothers land
pendicle	small piece of land detached from the main holding
penny wedding	wedding at which the guests contributed towards the food and drink.
pertinents	everything belonging to and part of the lands being conveyed
Pinkie Cleugh battle of	10 September 1547; near Mussleburgh. Scottish army of 23,000 commanded by Arran and Huntly routed by English army which utilised naval gunfire. Estimated 10,000 Scots casualties
pit and gallows	the right of execution
plack	Scots coin valued at 4 Scots pennies. (see currency)
plaid	rectangular length of woven cloth, usually tartan, worn as an outer garment
plenishings	furniture
ploughgate	old Scots land measurement
policies	enclosed grounds around a country house
port	town or castle gateway or entrance
portioner	owner of a portion of land once part of a larger estate, small feu

precentor	person appointed by the Kirk Session to lead the singing in Presbyterian churches; in early times he was often also the school master
precept	warrant or authority from a feudal superior for an infeftment
precognition	statement of a witness, taken before the trial begins
presbyterian	system in which the church is governed by elders
presbytery	ecclesiastical court above the kirk session and below the synod
Proclamation of Banns	public statement of the intention to be married
pro Indiviso	undivided, jointly, in common
procurator	lawyer or agent.
proprietory toun	fermtoun in which some of the inhabitants were also owners.
proport	convey
Protocol Book	book used by a notary to record his instruments.
provost	chief magistrate of the burgh:
pupil	school child: in law child under the age of minority, girl under 12, boy under 14

R

regiment	a regiment is simply a parent organisation and has no tactical function. Prior to the start of WW1 a regiment had either one or two battalions. In war time these are expanded and a regiment may have 20 or more battalions, hence 5th Battalion Seaforth Highlanders or 15th Battalion H.L.I. Traditionally, each regiment had its own county or town affiliations and generally recruited from that area. Regimental Headquarters may be permanently based in a town within the affiliated area. Cavalry and artillery regiments are broadly similar
relict	widow
rig	strip of cultivated land
room and kitchen	tenement dwelling; a flat with two rooms, a kitchen/ livingroom with a bed recess and a separate bed room
roods	measure of land. (see weights and measures)
roup	sell or let at a public auction
Royal Highland Fusiliers	regiment came into being in 1959 with the amalgamation of the Royal Scots Fusiliers and The Highland Light Infantry. Now part of the Scottish Lowland Division
Royal Scots	regiment raised in 1633, the oldest regiment in the British army. Now part of the Scottish Lowland Division.
Royal Scots Fusiliers	the oldest fusilier regiment it was raised in 1678, amalgamated in 1959 with the Highland Light Infantry to form the Royal Highland Fusiliers
Roy's Map	begun after the Battle of Culloden, the military survey of Scotland is named after General William Roy, the chief surveyor. Drawn to scale of 1 inch to 4000 yards, it is relatively well detailed, showing rivers, mountains, towns, villages and roads. The original is held at the British Museum in London
runrig	system of cultivation; joint land holding where disjoined strips of land were allocated in rotation to tenants

S

sark	shirt
sarking	roof boards
sasine	infeftment ; act of giving legal possession of land
saugh	willow rods, willow wood, a rope made of twisted willow withes.
Scots	acceptable form in Scottish Standard English to describe a person born in Scotland, as opposed to 'Scotch' which would be correct when applied to whisky or broth
Scots Guards	regiment raised in 1639 as a guard for King Charles I ;now part of the Household Division
Seaforth Highlanders	regiment raised in 1778 as the 78th later 72nd of Foot by the Earl of Seaforth: amalgamated in 1961 with the Queen's Own Cameron Highlanders to form the 'Queen's Own Highlanders' (Seaforth and Camerons) Lately amalgamated again with the Gordon Highlanders to form 'The Highlanders' (Seaforth, Gordons and Camerons); now part of the Scottish Highland Division
secession	departure from the Church of Scotland by a group of ministers in 1723, led by Ebenezer and Ralph Erskine

sergeant	in a Sheriffdom, the officer whose duty it was to arrest and incarcerate offenders: infantry sergeant, second in command of a platoon of 30-35 men
shieling	summer pasture in the hills
shilling	silver coin the weight of 12 silver pennies: classification of the strength of beer e.g. 70 shilling ale
shilling land	land of which the annual product was valued at a shilling under the auld extent
shod	provided with shoes
souter	cobbler
spale basket	a basket made of woven strips of oak, ash or hazel wood
statistical account	a series of three accounts of the parish written by its minister. The first two 1791-1799 (old) and 1839-1845 (new or second) are particularly useful for the Scottish family historian. Although the quality varies from parish to parish, they generally provide a wonderful snapshot of life in that parish at the time and are a 'must read' for anyone who can identify an ancestor as living in the parish at the time. Covers over 900 Scottish parishes. A 3rd Statistical Account produced in the 1960s
statute labour	certain amount of day's work on roads required from tenants cottars and labourers
steading	farm buildings: once the farm itself
stent	assessment, tax
sterling	English money
superior	a grantor of land to another, who then become his vassal in return for payment of feu-duty
Sutherland Highlanders	regiment raised in 1800 as the 93rd of Foot. Linked in 1881 with the Argyllshire Highlanders to form the 2nd battalion Princess Louise's Argyll and Sutherland Highlanders. The old 93rd were the famous 'Thin Red Line' of Balaclava fame

T

tack	lease; tenancy, especially the leasehold of a farm
tacksman	holder of a substantial lease
tail	entourage or retinue of a nobleman or Highland chief
tenant at will	having no security of tenure; occupying at the landlord's pleasure
thirlage	the requirement for a tenant to grind his grain at a particular mill; remained a legal practice until 1777
tolbooth	burgh jail
toll	something paid as a duty; checkpoint on a toll road
toun	settlement with its buildings and the immediate area

V

vassal	person who holds land from a feudal superior
victual	food, provisions

W

wadset	pledge of lands or other heritable property as security (conveyed by sasine) but with the right of recovery on payment of the debt: mortgage
Whitsunday	Scottish quarter day: term-day 15 May; date for removals and employing servants. Changed in 1886 to 28 May
wright	carpenter; person involved in making something

Y

yaird/yerd	cottage or kitchen garden

WEIGHTS AND MEASURES

A great deal of diversity and confusion reigned within early Scottish weights and measures. Various official attempts failed to improve matters until 1661 when a parliamentary commission recommended the setting up of national standards. Various burghs were chosen as custodians of the exemplars, Edinburgh received the *ell* for all lineal measure, the *jug* for liquid capacity was to be kept by Stirling, Linlithgow the *firlot* for dry measure and the *troy stone* for weight was kept by Lanark. Generally, these standard weights and measures were adhered to, with some irregularities, particularly in dry measure. In 1824, statutory weights and measures were established throughout the United Kingdom and gradually adhered to. Some of the old names were adopted as fractions of the new imperial hundred weight.

WEIGHTS

1. According to the standard of Lanark for TROY weight:

SCOTS	AVOIRDUPOIS	METRIC WEIGHT
1 drop	1.093 drams	1. 921 grammes
16 drops = 1 ounce 1 oz.	1.5 drams	31 grammes
16 ounces = 1 pound	1 lb. 1 oz. 8 drams	496 grammes
16 pounds = 1 stone	17 lbs. 8 oz	7.936 kilogrammes

2. According to the standard of Edinburgh for TRON weight:

SCOTS	AVOIRDUPOIS	METRIC WEIGHT
1 drop	1.378 drams	2.4404 grammes
16 drops = 1 ounce	1 oz. 6 drams	39.04 grammes
16 ounces = 1 pound	1 lb. 6 oz. 1 dram	624.74 grammes
16 pounds = 1 stone	1 stone 8 lbs. 1 oz.	9.996 kilogrammes

CAPACITY

Liquid measure according to the standard of Stirling (Jug)

SCOTS	IMPERIAL	METRIC
1 gill	.749 gill	.053 litres
4 gills = 1 MUTCHKIN	2.996 gills	.212 litres
2 mutchkins = 1 CHOPIN	2 pints 3.984 gills	1.696 litres
8 pints = 1 gallon	3 gallons .25 gills	3.638 litres
1 pint = 104. 2034 Imp. cub. ins.	1 pint = 34.659 Imp. cub. ins	1 litre = 61.027 cub ins.

Dry measure according to the standard of Linlithgow

1. For wheat, peas, beans, meal etc.

SCOTS	IMPERIAL	METRIC
1 lippie (or FORPET)	.499 gallons	2.268 litres
4 lippies = 1 PECK	1.996 gallons	9.072 litres
4 pecks = 1FIRLOT	3 pecks 1.986 gallons	36.286 litres
4 firlots = 1 BOLL	3 bushels 3 pecks 1.944 galls	145.145 litres
16 bolls = 1 CHALDER	7 quarters 7 bushels 3 pecks 1.07 galls	2322. 324 litres
1 firlot = 2214.322 cub. ins	1 gallon = 277.274 cub. ins.	1 litre = 61.027 cub. ins.

2. For barley, oats and malt

1 lippie (or forpet)	728 gallons	3.037 litres
4 lippies = 1 peck	peck .912 gallons	13.229 litres
4 pecks = 1 firlot	1 bushel 1 peck 1.650 gallons	52.916 litres
4 firlots = 1 boll	5 bushels 3 pecks .600 gallons	211.664 litres
16 bolls = 1 chalder	11 quarters 5 bushels 1.615	3386.624 litres
1 firlot = 3230.305 cub. in.	gallons	

LINEAR AND SQUARE MEASURES
According to the standard ELL of Edinburgh

Linear

1 inch	.0016 inches	2.54 centimetres
8.88 inches = 1 SCOTS link	8.8942 inches	22.55 centimetres
8.1 12 inches = 1 foot	12.0192 inches	30.5287 centimetres
3 1/12 feet = 1 ELL	37.0598 inches (11/37 yards)	94.1318 centimetres
6 ells = 1 fall (FA)	6.1766 yards (1.123 poles)	5.6479 metres
4 falls = 1 chain	24.7064 yards (1.123 chains)	22.5916 metres
10 chains = 1 furlong	247.064 yards (1.123 furlongs)	225.916 metres
8 furlongs = 1 mile	1976. 522 yards (1.123 miles)	1.8073 kilometres

Square

1 sq. inch	1.0256 sq. inch	6.4516 sq. centimetre
1 sq ell	1.059 sq. yards	.8853 sq. metre
36 sq. ells = 1 sq. fall	38.125 sq. yards (1 pole 7.9 sq	31.87 sq. metres
40 falls = 1 sq. rood	1525 sq. yards (1 rood 10 poles 13 sq. yards 12.7483 acres	
4 roods = 1 sq. acre	6100 sq. yards (1.26 acres)	5099 hectare

CURRENCY

Until the late 14th century the Scottish currency was roughly equivalent to that of England. It then began a slow, but steady decline against that of its neighbour, until by the end of the 16th century it was roughly 1/6. By the time of the union with England in 1707, it was only equivalent to 1/12. Officially the Scots currency ceased to exist, but many of the names of the coins continued to be used.

SCOTS	STERLING	DECIMAL
1 penny	1/12d	—
2 pennies = 1Bodle	1/6d	—
2 bodles = 1 Plack	1/3d	—
3 bodles = 1 Bawbee	1 halfpenny	—
2 bawbees = 1 Shilling	1 penny	.42 pence
13 shillings 4d = 1 Merk	1s 11½ pennies	5 1/2 pence
20 shillings = 1 Pound	1s 8d	8 pence

Reference Source List

Abbreviations

ASHRM   Argyll and Sutherland Highlanders Regimental Museum, The Castle, Stirling
B.L   British Library, London
C.E.B   Census Enumeration Book
G.R.O   General Register Office, Edinburgh
N.A.S   National Archives of Scotland, Edinburgh
N.L.S   National Library of Scotland, Edinburgh
N.S.A   New Statistical Account
O.S.A   Old Statistical Account
S.C.A.   Stirling Council Archives, Stirling
S.C.L   Stirling Central Library, Stirling

1. National Census Returns 1841-1891, S.C.L
2. Gargunnock Old Parish Registers, N.A.S.
3. Gargunnock Kirk Session Minutes Ref: CH2/1121/1-5, S.C.A.
4. Old Statistical Account Gargunnock Parish 1790, S.C.L
5. New Statistical Account Gargunnock Parish 1840, S.C.L
6. Third Statistical Account Gargunnock Parish 1960, S.C.L
7. Old Statistical Account Campsie Parish 1793. S.C.L
8. Disposition Gourley to McNair 1777, N.A.S
9. Disposition Abercromby to Gourley 1755, N.A.S
10. A View of the State of Agriculture in the County of Stirlingshire 1798, S.C.L
11. Hearth Tax Returns 1795, N.A.S
12. Disposition James McNair to John Murdoch 1796, N.A.S
13. Disposition Murdoch to McCulloch 1819, N.A.S
14. International Genealogical Index, S.C.L
15. Military Survey of Scotland (Roy's Map) 1755, B.L
16. Monumental Inscriptions in the East of Stirlingshire, S.C.L
17. Disposition McCulloch to McDonald 1823, N.A.S
18. Valuation Rolls for the County of Stirlingshire. S.C.A.
19. Ordnance Survey 25" map 1860 Gargunnock, N.L.S
20. Gargunnock Estate Plan, John S Stirling 1851, S.C.A.
21. Stirling Observer Advertisement Sale of Public House Gargunnock 1900, S.C.A.
22. Stirling Saturday Observer 26 October 1901, page 4, S.C.A.
23. Stirling Observer September 1857 page 1, S.C.A.
24. Soldiers died in the Great War CD ROM. The Naval and Military Press Ltd 1998
25. Commonwealth Graves Commission Internet Database
26. Fasti Scotteuim Presbytery of Stirling pages 307 - 309, S.C.L
27. Gargunnock Kirk Session Accounts. Ref: Ch2/1121/8-10, S.C.A.
28. Presbytery of Stirling Records 1615 - 1630, S.C.A.
29. Ordnance Survey Name Books Ref: RH 4/23/187 Book 14, N.A.S
30. Inland Revenue Field Books (Ref IRS84/184, Assessment nos. 29, 102-3) N.A.S
31. Inland Revenue (Ordnance Survey) Maps (Ref IRS130/25 & 92), N.A.S
32. Chartulary of Gargunnock Estate, S.C.A.
33. Moir of Leckie Estate Papers, S.C.A.
34. Campbell of Ardkinlass Estate Papers, S.C.A.
35. Seton of Touch Papers, S.C.A.
36. Stirling of Gargunnock Estate Papers, S.C.A.

References

1. O.S.A. County of Stirling, *Parish of Gargunnock,* page 354. S.C.L
2. O.S.A County of Stirling, *Parish of Campsie,* page 269. S.C.L
3. Report by Birlawmen of Leckie dated 11 Nov 1813. *Moir of Leckie papers.* S.C.A.
4. Grassom's Map of Stirlingshire, 1817; S.C.A.
5. Register of the Great Seal, vol III, no 981. S.C.A
6. Ancient Castles and Mansions of Stirling Nobility, page 351. S.C.A
7. O.S.A. County of Stirling, *Parish of Gargunnock* page 352. S.C.L
8. Earl of Mar, family papers 1624. N.A.S

9. O.S.A. County of Stirling, *Parish of Gargunnock* page 352. S.C.L
10. Proceedings of the Society of Antiquities of Scotland, Vol. xci, 1957-8. Edinburgh
11. Stirlingshire Retours March 1555. S.C.A
12. Privy Council Register ,ii, 612. N.A.S
13. Lockhart Papers, ii. 487 and Glimpses of Church Life in Old Days, page 12. S.C.A
14. N.S.A. County of Stirling, *Parish of Gargunnock*, page 144. S.C.L
15. Robert Louis Stevenson and the Scottish Highlanders, page 57. S.C.L
16. The Forty Five (The last Jacobite Rebellion) page 84
17. Act of parliament James VI, 1606, page 346. S.C.A
18. Glimpses of Church Life in Old Days, page 5. S.C.A
19. Gargunnock Kirk Session Minutes, Sept 1626, Ref *CH2/1121/1-5*. S.C.A.
20. Gargunnock Kirk Session Minutes, Sept 1626, Ref *CH2/1121/1-5*. S.C.A.
21. Gargunnock Kirk Session Minutes, Aug 1631, Ref *CH2/1121/1-5*. S.C.A.
22. Gargunnock Kirk Session Minutes, Dec 1628, Ref *CH2/1121/1-5*. S.C.A.
23. Gargunnock Kirk Session Minutes, July 1631,Ref *CH2/1121/1-5*. S.C.A.
24. O.S.A. County of Stirling, *Parish of Gargunnock* page 367. S.C.L
25. Regimental History of the Covenanting Armies, 1639 - 1651, page 292
26. Gargunnock Kirk Session Minutes, Jan 1645, Ref *CH2/1121/1-5*. S.C.A.
27. History of Stirlingshire, Volume 1 (Nimmo) page 220. S.C.L
28. Fasti Scotteuim Presbytery of Stirling page 307, S.C.L
29. Gargunnock Kirk Session Minutes, Oct-Nov 1652, Ref *CH2/1121/1-5*. S.C.A.
30. Gargunnock Kirk Session Minutes, 1654, Ref *CH2/1121/1-5*. S.C.A.
31. Gargunnock Kirk Session Minutes, Nov 1652, Ref *CH2/1121/1-5*. S.C.A.
32. Gargunnock Kirk Session Minutes, 1652, Ref *CH2/1121/1-5*. S.C.A.
33. Gargunnock Kirk Session Minutes, Jan 1656, Ref *CH2/1121/1-5*. S.C.A.
34. Gargunnock Kirk Session Minutes, Jan 1656, Ref *CH2/1121/1-5*. S.C.A.
35. Gargunnock Kirk Session Minutes, June1646, Ref *CH2/1121/1-5*. S.C.A.
36. Gargunnock Kirk Session Minutes, June1646, Ref *CH2/1121/1-5*. S.C.A.
37. Gargunnock Kirk Session Minutes, Aug 1625, Ref *CH2/1121/1-5*. S.C.A.
38. The Concise Scots Dictionary, Scottish Currency, Weights and Measures, page 817. S.C.L
39. Gargunnock Kirk Session Minutes, May 1626, Ref *CH2/1121/1-5*. S.C.A.
40. Gargunnock Kirk Session Minutes, July 1631, Ref *CH2/1121/1-5*. S.C.A.
41. Gargunnock Kirk Session Minutes, May 1626, Ref *CH2/1121/1-5*. S.C.A.
42. Gargunnock Kirk Session Minutes, Sept 1659, Ref *CH2/1121/1-5*. S.C.A.
43. O.S.A. County of Stirling, *Parish of Gargunnock* page 366. S.C.L
44. Gargunnock Kirk Session Minutes, 1646 Ref *CH2/1121/1-5*. S.C.A.
45. Gargunnock Kirk Session Minutes, Feb 1626, Ref *CH2/1121/1-5*. S.C.A.
46. O.S.A. County of Stirling, *Parish of Gargunnock* page 364. S.C.L
47. O.S.A. County of Stirling, *Parish of Gargunnock* page 365-367. S.C.L
48. Fasti Scotteuim, *Presbytery of Stirling* page 308, S.C.L
49. Fasti Scotteuim, *Presbytery of Stirling* page 308, S.C.L
50. Scotland's Story, page 140
51. Stirling Burgh Records 1695. S.C.A
52. Stirling of Gargunnock estate papers. S.C.A
53. Act of Parliament James VI, 1606. S.C.A
55. O.S.A. County of Stirling, *Parish of Gargunnock*, page 362, S.C.L
56. O.S.A. County of Stirling, *Parish of Gargunnock*, page 362, S.C.L
57. Gargunnock Estate papers, *Gargunnock Chartulary*, *Volumes I and II*. S.C.A
58. O.S.A. County of Stirling, *Parish of Gargunnock*, page 370, S.C.L
59. Gargunnock Kirk Session Records March1655. Ref *Ch2/1121/1-5*. S.C.A
60. The Royal Commission on Ancient and Historical Monuments of Scotland, *Stirlingshire Vol 2, para 453*. S.C.A
61. Disposition James McNair to Wm Murdoch 3rd June 1796. Ref Pr 34.346. N.A.S
62. O.S.A. County of Stirling, *Parish of Gargunnock*, page 362. S.C.L
63. Leckie Estate Papers, Disposition Leckie/ Moir. S.C.A
64. O.S.A. County of Stirling, Parish of Gargunnock, page 362. S.C.L
65. Ancient Castles and Mansions of Stirling Nobility, page 354 - 356. S.C.A
66. Burke's Peerage and Baronetage, Argyll. 1928 Editon, page 133. S.C.A
67. Ancient Castles and Mansions of Stirling Nobility, page 354 - 356. S.C.A

68. Disposition McNair / Murdoch June 1796. Private collection of author
69. Disposition Gourley / McNair November 1777. Private collection of author
70. Disposition McNair / Murdoch June 1796. Private collection of author
71. O.S.A. County of Stirling, Parish of Gargunnock. S.C.L
72. O.S.A. County of Stirling, Parish of Gargunnock. S.C.L
73. Acts of the Parliament of Scotland 1641, 1661, 1685. N.A.S
74. O.S.A. County of Stirling, Parish of Gargunnock. S.C.L
75. O.S.A. County of Stirling, Parish of Gargunnock. S.C.L
76. The Stirling Advertiser, 4th December 1829. S.C.A.
77. Gargunnock Kirk Session Minutes, Lair Books 1760, Ref *CH2/1121/1-5*. S.C.A.
78. Gargunnock Kirk Session Minutes, Lair Books 1760, Ref *CH2/1121/1-5*. S.C.A.
79. O.S.A. County of Stirling, Parish of Gargunnock, S.C.L
80. Disposition McNair / Murdoch June 1796. Private collection of author
81. O.S.A. County of Stirling, Parish of Gargunnock, S.C.L
82. O.S.A. County of Stirling, Parish of Gargunnock, S.C.L
84. O.S.A. County of Stirling, Parish of Gargunnock, S.C.L
85. O.S.A. County of Stirling, Parish of Gargunnock, S.C.L
86. O.S.A. County of Stirling, Parish of Gargunnock, S.C.L
87. A General view of the state of Agriculture in Stirlingshire (Beeches) 1798. S.C.L
88. A General view of the state of Agriculture in Stirling (Beeches) 1798. Page 47. S.C.L
89. Disposition McNair / Murdoch June 1796. Private collection of author
90. Gargunnock O.P.R, (Births) Sept 1803, S.C.A
91. Disposition Murdoch / McCulloch May 1819. Private collection of author
92. Roads and Bridges (Scotland) Act 1878. S.C.A
93. Instrument of Sasine McCulloch / MacDonald June 1823. Private collection of author
94. Instrument of Sasine McCulloch / McCulloch 26 October 1853. Private collection of author
95. Gargunnock Kirk Session Minutes 1826, Ref *CH2/1121/1-5*. S.C.A.
96. O.S.A. County of Stirling, Parish of Gargunnock, page 375, S.C.L
97. Deed of Novodamus, John Stirling Stirling / Wm McNair 1890. Stirling of Gargunnock Estate Papers S.C.A
98. Old and New Statistical Accounts, County of Stirling, Parish of Gargunnock, S.C.L
99. Whisky Distillers of U.K 1887, Stirling of Gargunnock Estate papers, S.C.A
100. Minutes of the Stirling Board of Health 1831-32, S.C.A
101. Minutes of the Stirling Board of Health 1831-32, S.C.A
102. Stirling Journal, 9th February 1832. S.C.A.
103. Stirling Advertiser, 10th August 1832. S.C.A
104. People and Society in Scotland. Volume II, 1830-1814, chapter 1, page 23
105. Gargunnock O.P.R (births/bapt) May 1832. Ref 481/1-2 S.C.A
106. Deed of Novodamus, John Stirling Stirling / Wm McNair 1890. Stirling of Gargunnock Estate Papers. S.C.A
107. Stirling Advertiser, 17th August 1832. S.C.A
109. Stirling (The Royal Burgh) page 173. S.C.L
110. Fasti Scotteuim, *Presbytery of Stirling* page 308, S.C.L
111. N.S.A. County of Stirling, Parish of Gargunnock, page 58, S.C.L
112. Third Statistical Account, County of Stirling, Parish of Gargunnock, page 114. S.C.L
113. Ordnance Survey Name Books. Ref: *RH 4/23/187 Book 14*, N.A.S
114. Disposition and Settlement. *McCulloch / McCulloch 1849*. Private collection of author.
115. Gargunnock O.P.R (deaths) Apr 1847. Ref 481/1-2. S.C.A
116. Gargunnock O.P.R (marriages) June 1830. Ref 481/1-2. S.C.A
117. Stirling Valuation Roll 1855, *Gargunnock Parish*, page 93. S.C.A
118. Roll Book 93rd Highlanders 1820. ASHRM, Stirling Castle, Stirling
119. Records of the 93rd Highlanders 1823-34. ASHRM, Stirling Castle, Stirling
120. Gargunnock O.P.R (marriages) Nov 1848. Ref *481/1-2*. S.C.A
121. C.E.B. Gargunnock 1851. *Dist No 482, book 1*, page 8. S.C.L
122. Disposition *McCulloch / Forsyth May 1866*. Private collection of author
123. C.E.B. Gargunnock 1851. *Dist No 481, book 1, page 15*. S.C.L
124. Gargunnock Estate Papers (Chartulary), Ref *Old No. 2/1*. S.C.A
125. Slaters Trade Directory of Stirling 1860, S.C.A
126. C.E.B. Gargunnock 1861. *Dist 481, book 2, page 5*. S.C.L

127. Valuation Roll 1865, *County of Stirlingshire, Gargunnock Parish*, page 115. S.C.A
128. Ordnance Survey Name Books Ref: *RH 4/23/187 Book 14*, N.A.S
129. Gargunnock Estate Papers (Chartulary), Ref *Old No.2, New No1*. S.C.A
130. Fasti Scotteuim, *Presbytery of Stirling pages 307 - 309*, S.C.L
131. Ordnance Survey Field Books, Ref *RH4/23/187 Book 14*. N.A.S.
132. Deed of Novodamus, *John Stirling Stirling / Wm McNair 1890*, Stirling Estate Papers. S.C.A
133. Gargunnock Estate Papers, *Accounts of the Gargunnock Clothing Club 1870*. S.C.A
134. Third Statistical Account. *The County of Stirling, Parish of Gargunnock, page 144*. S.C.L
135. C.E.B. Gargunnock 1871. *Dist 481, book 1*. S.C.L
136. Third Statistical Account. *The County of Stirling, Parish of Gargunnock, page 145*. S.C.L
137. Family Papers in the possession of Mr John McLaren, Gargunnock
138. Kincardine Parish O.P.R (births). G.R.O
139. Valuation Rolls 1865, County of Stirlingshire, *Gargunnock Parish, page 115*. S.C.A
140. C.E.B. Gargunnock 1871. *Dist No 481, book 2, page 10*. S.C.L
141. Local Tradition (Miss E Patterson, Gargunnock) 2000
142. Statutory Records (Marriages) 1880, Ref *362 Entry No 16*. New Register House, Edinburgh
143. Statutory Records (Births) 1887, Ref *418A Entry No 25*. New Register House, Edinburgh
144. C.E.B. Gargunnock 1871. *Dist No 481, book 1*, page 2. S.C.L
145. Statutory Records (Marriages) 1878, Ref *490 Entry No 126*. New Register House, Edinburgh
146. C.E.B. Gargunnock 1881. *Dist No 481, book 1*, page 2. S.C.L
147. Disposition Brown / Brown May 1884. Private collection of author
148. Statutory Records (Deaths) 1900. Ref *362 Entry No 16*. New Register House, Edinburgh
149. Gargunnock Kirk Session Minutes May 1894, Ref *CH2/1121/1-5*. S.C.A.
150. Stirling Advertiser, *19th October 1900*. S.C.A
151. Disposition Brown / Stevenson / Brown Douglas, November 1900. Private collection of author
152. Stirling Saturday Observer, *26 October 1901*, page 4. S.C.A
153. Fasti Scotteuim, *Presbytery of Stirling pages 307 - 309*, S.C.L
154. Statutory Records (deaths) 1988, Ref *481 Entry No 3*. New Register House, Edinburgh
155. Fasti Scotteuim, *Presbytery of Stirling pages 307 - 309*, S.C.L
156. Gargunnock Parish Magazine March 1947. S.C.A
157. C.E.B, St Stephen's, Edinburgh 1881. Ref. *685-1, book 104, page 17*. R.G.O
158. Stirling Journal and Advertiser, *6th November 1903, page 8*. S.C.A.
159. Disposition Stevenson / Brown Douglas to the Minister of Gargunnock in trust February 1910. Private collection of the author
160. Stirling Journal and Advertiser, *March 25, 1910. Page 2*. S.C.A.
161. Stirling Journal and Advertiser, *March 25, 1910. Page 2*. S.C.A.
162. Stirling Journal and Advertiser, *March 25, 1910. Page 2*. S.C.A.
163. Inland Revenue Field Books. Ref. *IRS 84/183, assessment no 29*. N.A.S.
164. Inland Revenue Field Books. Ref. *IRS 84/184, assessment no 102*. N.A.S.
165. Soldier's Died in the Great War. CD ROM Naval and Military Press. S.C.L
166. Gargunnock Estate Papers. *Gargunnock House Leases 1914 - 1920*. S.C.A
167. Valuation Rolls 1916/17, *County of Stirling, Parish of Gargunnock, page 65*. S.C.A
168. Disposition Brown Douglas / Stevenson to Elder McDonald March 1927. Private collection of author

Bibliography

1. Bailey G.W. *Falkirk or Paradise,* John Donald Publishers, Edinburgh 1996
2. Cage R.A., *Scottish Poor Laws 1745-1845,* Scottish Academic Press 1981
3. Chambers R, *History of the Rebellion of 1745,* W & R Chamber, London and Edinburgh 1840
4. Devine T and Mitchison R (Eds), *People and Society in Scotland 1760-1830,* John Donald Publishers Edinburgh 1988
5. Devine T. (Ed), *Farm Servants and Labour in Lowland Scotland, 1770-1914* Edinburgh 1984
6. Dickson N. *The Kirk and Its Worthies,* Foulis London & Edinburgh 1912
7. Fleming J.S. *Ancient Castles and Mansions of Stirling Nobility,* 1902
8. Furgol E. A *Regimental History of the Covenanting Armies* John Donald Publishers Edinburgh 1990
9. Fraser W.H and Morris R.J *People and Society in Scotland Vol II 1830-1914,* John Donald Edinburgh 1995.
10. Graham D. *Metrical History of the Rebellion 1745,* 1st Edition, Glasgow, 1746
11. Graham Henry G. *Social Life in Scotland in the 18th Century,* Black, London 1906
12. Haldane E. S. *The Scotland of Our Fathers,* Alex MacLehose & Co London 1933
13. Henderson D. *Highland Soldier,* John Donald Publishers Edinburgh 1989
14. Hook M and Ross W. *The Forty Five (The Last Jacobite Rebellion)* HMSO.
15. Jarrett D. *Britain 1688 - 1815.* Longmans Green & Co. London 1968
16. Levitt I and Smout C. *The State of the Scottish Working Class in 1843,* Scottish Academic Press Edinburgh 1979
17. Lawson L, (Ed), *Jacobites in Stirlingshire,* Nelson & Sons, 1971
18. Mair C. *Stirling The Royal Burgh,* John Donald Publishers Edinburgh 1995
19. McNeil Horton Rev J . H. *Glimpses of Church List in Old Days,* Learmouth & Son, Stirling 1930
20. Morris David B. *Robert Louis Stevenson and the Scottish Highlanders,* 1929
21. Nimmo Wm. *The History of Stirlingshire,* 2 Vols, 3rd Ed, Thos D Morrison, Glasgow 1880
22. Robinson M. (Editor in Chief) *The Concise Scots Dictionary,* Chambers Edinburgh 1996
23. Steven M. *Parish Life in Eighteenth Century Scotland,* Scottish Cultural Press Aberdeen 1995
24. Stevenson D, *Scottish Covenanters and Irish Confederates,* The Ulster Historical Foundation 1981
25. Smout T.C. *A History of the Scottish People 1560-1830.* Wm Collins, Sons & Co Glasgow 1969
26. Smout T.C. *A History of the Scottish people 1830-1950,* Harper/Collins Fontana Press Glasgow.
27. Steel T. *Scotland's Story,* Fontana / Collins London 1984
28. Various. Edited by Devine T M, Mitchison R, Dodgson R A. *Land and Society in Early Scotland,* Clarendon Press Oxford 1981
29. Various. *The Gazetteer of Scotland Vol 1 A-H,* Fullerton & Co Edinburgh & London
30. Whyte I. *Agriculture and Society in Seventeenth Century Scotland,* John Donald. Edinburgh 1979
31. Whyte I. *Scotland's Society and Economy in Transition c.1500- c1760,* McMillan Press Ltd 1997